THE
RITE OF
PASSAGE

Describing the
Spiritual Rites of Passage of
Rev. Jay J. Samonie, Ph.D.

The Rite of Passage:
Describing the
Spiritual Rites of Passage of
Rev. Jay J. Samonie, Ph.D.

© 2006
Rev. Jay J. Samonie, Ph.D.

Library of Congress Control Number: 2006910790

ISBN: 978-0-9752636-2-4

Art work on cover design: from a painting
by Rev. Jay J. Samonie.
"Stairway to Heaven"

this and other works available at
www.fatherjay.org

Illustrations at start of each chapter sketched by
Rev. Jay J. Samonie

Printed in the USA by Morris Publishing
3212 East Highway 30 • Kearney NE 68847
(800) 650-7888

BOOKS BY THE SAME AUTHOR

On My Way Home

Reflections on My Way Home

My Greatest Joys on My Way Home

The Holy Spirit: Our Divine Companion
Guiding Us On Our Way Home

A STATEMENT BY THE AUTHOR

There is no attempt to write anything contrary to Catholic Belief in this book. I am merely recording my mystical and spiritual experiences, which were very real, overwhelming and rare enough to become the content of my fifth book.

DEDICATION

This book is dedicated to my brother Tony, who was called to the Heavenly World of Spirit after a brief illness.

ACKNOWLEDGMENTS

Richard and Kathy Rice for helping me to arrange my book for publication.

Jack and Ronnie Morgan for proof-reading this book.

Sally Owen for assisting me in gathering information for this book.

NOTES BY THE AUTHOR

After my fourth published book, "The Holy Spirit: Our Divine Companion Guiding Us On Our Way Home", I had another book in mind which was almost ready for publishing. It was a book on the legacy of a great psychic of our modern age...Edgar Cayce. The book was almost entirely written about four years ago. It was not ready yet for publication, but needed some editing, and actual rewriting. I had been trying to do this unsuccessfully, for the last three months. Every time I began editing that book, something stopped me. My mind became, in a sense, blocked and I would again put it aside; however, something very unusual happened to me that changed my direction. What inspired me by giving me the title and the contents of this book is described in

detail in the first chapter. I consider it a
Divine Mandate to write my fifth book called
"The Rite of Passage." I believe you will, too,
when you begin reading this book.

CONTENTS

CONTENTS

Jacab Samonie, Sr., Tony Samonie and Mary Samonie
Father Jay's father, brother and mother

CHAPTER 1
THE INSPIRATION TO WRITE THIS BOOK.

At four o'clock in the morning on May 13, 2006, a Voice spoke loudly enough to wake me from a deep sleep. Without hesitation, the Voice said, "My son, you are writing the wrong book!" I had no doubt that it was the Voice of my Lord and Master Jesus. By this time, I had come to know that Voice quite well.

I was half asleep, but I still managed to ask, "Lord Jesus, how can I be writing the wrong book?"

"It's not that the book is wrong, my son, but the timing is not right to produce a book on Edgar Cayce; it can be laid aside for a while. For now, I suggest that you begin writing a book on the *Rite of Passage.*"

I naturally questioned: "*The Rite of Passage?* I am not even sure that I know what it means; and besides, what does that have to do with me at my age? When and where do I begin?"

"Your book will be called THE RITE OF PASSAGE, *describing the Spiritual Rites of Passage of Rev. Jay Samonie.*"

"If you haven't noticed, all your life, since you were a young child, working openly and verbally with the Holy Spirit, we have put you in contact with certain famous people or had you read about other people's experiences or theories which had a profound impact on your life. Every time your values changed or you experienced even the slightest enlightenment, it was a Spiritual Rite of Passage for you."

"Did that happen a lot?"

"Oh, yes!" I was told. "Get out of bed for a moment and find a pencil and a blank sheet of paper. There were many more incidents that took place but We are going to give you twenty such occasions that changed your values and convictions in a world filled with distractions. Every time your awareness was either expanded or elevated, you experienced another *Spiritual Rite of Passage*. None of these experiences was a coincidence. You were being led very carefully to your present awareness...which is the highest awareness of Truth, Reality, Knowledge and the Purpose of Life you have ever achieved in your spiritual development."

I was completely overwhelmed by all the attention the Lord Jesus and the Holy Spirit were giving to me. They even mentioned more than once that there were Angels and Saints also assisting them.

I then realized that I was being guided to write this fifth book by responding to the many extraordinary events in my life and recording them in book form.

"Your life has also been watched over and protected very carefully so that you could experience these Spiritual Rites of Passage." The Lord Jesus continued, "Have you forgotten how many times your life was at the point of death…and you did not cross over into the world of spirit?"

Reflecting on what He had just said, I sat in meditation and began to open my *memory banks*, reviewing my life history! Some of those experiences were not easily forgotten and so I remembered them well. When I was six years old, I was hit in the back of the head by a motorcycle as the driver was illegally turning on a red light. The handle bar of the motorcycle knocked me at least twenty feet in the air before I landed on the pavement. (I was actually coming home from school, innocently crossing the street on a green light.)

I was unconscious for a long time and my parents and siblings were standing around the hospital bed not knowing whether I was going to live or to die. I suddenly opened my eyes, was conscious and feeling fine. The family was happily surprised! The doctors were also surprised and checked me over carefully. Their conclusion: It was miraculous! I was in a stable healthy condition: no bones broken, no concussion and ready to go home. That was my first brush with death.

When I was a Deacon, a year before ordination to the priesthood and during a tornado warning, I was in a cabin praying with Mexican migrant workers. One of the migrant workers saw a tornado through the window and was terrified! I looked out the window myself and saw the funnel of the tornado coming straight at us. The tornado was tearing up everything in its path. There were frightening green clouds above it, another sign of an active tornado. We prayed hard! Our very souls were crying out for help! Just before the tornado struck our little cabin, it was as if the very Power of Almighty God, like *A Divine Hand* that gently lifted us in the air and moved us about 400 feet to the side so that we escaped certain death. Only a Divine Power could have saved us that day...again. I believe it was the Power of Lord Jesus and the Holy Spirit. He said clearly that they were keeping me alive to experience my spiritual Rites of Passage.

As a young priest, I was driving from Detroit to Chicago with a classmate, Joe Brady, for a weekend vacation in the Windy City. It was winter and we suddenly skidded over some black ice which was not possible to see in advance. We were headed toward a huge ditch and I thought for sure we would die on impact. We said "our goodbyes" to one another.

Unfortunately, it appeared that we were both destined to die at a young age! Instead, we somehow hit an unseen guard rail which apparently popped up out of nowhere by the side of the road. The car was damaged on impact, but was still in a condition to be driven. It was miraculous that we escaped death. We had the car repaired while we enjoyed our weekend in Chicago.

Through the many years of driving, I was involved in a few car accidents. On the freeways, those accidents could easily have turned out to be fatal. I continued to survive without injury!

I was gifted with good health and enjoyed Divine protection most of my life. However, beginning in July of 2004, I began to live on the edge of life and death. I felt strongly that I was being called to cross over into the afterlife and finally taken Home. I was seventy-four years old at that time. Every book I have written addresses the experience of dying and going Home to be in the Heavenly Realm with God.

This was it! My time had come! I was rushed by helicopter to St. Joseph Mercy Hospital in Ann Arbor, Michigan. There were about eight or nine doctors in white coats waiting at the helicopter pad. They were notified in advance of the seriousness of my condition. The main artery going directly through my heart (called the L.A.D.) was 100 percent blocked. The doctors immediately began working on me with a catheter while I was being placed on a gurney, and without question, saved my life. I had another heart attack the following month and they rushed me to St. Joseph Hospital by helicopter a second time and the wonderful team of doctors saved my life again.

In the next seven months, I was rushed to Botsford hospital in Farmington, Michigan eight times with Congestive Heart Failure and survived each time. I did die after a very serious stroke in October of 2004. It appeared that the Lord Jesus and the Holy Spirit had finished their role as Heavenly Guides and it was time for me to experience death. I did experience death. I was perfectly happy to go Home, but the Lord Jesus suddenly appeared at my bedside and said it was not my time. I had already died and crossed over into a hospital on the other side. He sent me back into my motionless body which was like a corpse and said I would begin to recover. I am still recovering after being in the world of spirit on the other side. But I am still here! I guess I am one of those rare people who was sent back from the dead because there were still things to do and to experience before going Home.

I am humbled by the attention I have received from these Heavenly Sources, but please do not consider me an exception! I was also told that every person living on Planet Earth goes through certain Rites of Passage and protection against dying before they have completed their script or mission in this life. If my readers reflected on their life's events, I am sure they would recall a sign of God's protection on the freeway where they avoided being seriously injured or even killed, surviving a serious sickness or given a happy report by the doctor after some lab tests that could have gone the other way.

Everyone is helped whether they know it or not, but so many of us do not slow down in this busy world to hear the gentle and guiding Voice of the Holy Spirit. This is unfortunate, since Divine Action is never a coincidence...and never wrong!

Practically every religion in the world develops its own meaningful and significant traditions regarding an established Ceremony or Rite of Passage for a youngster who is approaching adulthood. Each Rite of

Passage is distinct, depending on the Belief System of the Church or community practicing its own concept of adulthood for the young members of its tribe or community.

The Rites of Passage may not be restricted to a religious community. Often, they are mere steps of growth for a normal life unfolding in time.

The dictionary describes a Rite of Passage as "A ritual associated with a crisis for an individual." This crisis may take the form of graduating from one grade to the next, getting married, changing a job, moving to a new home, going on an unforgettable vacation, experiencing a new relationship or being hurt by a broken one. Simply put, it could be any experience that results in a change. The change usually implies growth or enlightenment, though not necessarily. It could simply mean just growing up!

In this larger view, the Rite of Passage may be a *ritual* that marks a change in a person's social or sexual status. Rites of Passage are often ceremonies surrounding events such as childbirth, going through the sensitive age of *puberty*, coming of age as an adult, experiencing menopause or a serious change in values while attending a wedding or a funeral.

You can add such events as becoming a *debutante*, going to the High School Prom, a *quinceañera* (becoming a fifteen year old young lady among the Hispanic people), the first day of school, learning to ride a bicycle, having a first girlfriend or boyfriend, obtaining a driver's license, a first job, college graduation, old enough to purchase alcohol, first time living on one's own, the first rental of an apartment or the purchase of a house.

Then, there is the first child, an adult Baptism, First Communion, Confirmation, Bar Mitzvah and Bat Mitzvah, Dream quest for Aboriginals, Rumspringa among the Amish, Vision Quest in some Native American cultures, Initiation Rites, Masonic Rituals, or joining any of the Armed Forces.

In Spanish Universities of the Modern Age, like *Universidad Complutense* in Alcalá de Henares, upon completion of his or her studies, the student is submitted to a public questioning by the faculty, who could ask tricky questions. If the student passed, he is invited by the professors and school mates to a party. This is a pleasing Rite of Passage. If the student fails, he would be publicly paraded through town with donkey ears. The result: a disturbing Rite of Passage. Any one time or another we all face a Rite of Passage which *occasionally forces* a change in awareness.

Fr. Solanus Casey

CHAPTER 2
REMEMBERING MY FIRST
SPIRITUAL RITE OF PASSAGE

My own spiritual Rites of Passage began
when I was a very young child. As far back
as I can remember, I seemed to have the

most incredible and spiritual experiences. At other times, I felt literally guided to meet certain famous and highly gifted people. The result was always the same: My views of God, my religious convictions and my values about life and death changed... sometimes, radically!

I believe that my first spiritual Rite of Passage took place when I was four or five years old. I grew up a couple of blocks from St. Bonaventure, a Franciscan Monastery located on the lower East side of Detroit, Michigan. One of its monks was the famous and saintly Fr. Solanus Casey. My parents owned a large grocery store close to the Monastery.

Fr. Solanus, who apparently was in charge of the kitchen at the time, would come often to my parents' store to purchase vegetables, fruits and other perishable foods when the Monastery kitchen ran short. Through these visits to the grocery store, Fr. Solanus knew my parents and the family quite well. I would later be an altar boy serving his Mass when he helped at Our Lady of Sorrows Church, also located on the lower east side of Detroit.

I knew, as a personal witness, that God's ability to heal is unlimited and always ready to heal through one of His chosen ones, such as Fr. Solanus Casey.

SO MY FIRST SPIRITUAL RITE OF PASSAGE BEGAN EVEN BEFORE I WAS SEVEN YEARS OF AGE! I NOW HAD FIRST-HAND EVIDENCE THAT HEALING WAS NOT ONLY POSSIBLE BUT A REALITY. At least three of my family members and relatives were healed by this remarkable man. People came from all parts of the country and also from overseas just to see him and hopefully to experience a healing. I do not think the average 4 or 5 year old has any knowledge of healing. I did, and so did other children who lived near the Monastery.

Yet, life was not easy for Fr. Solanus. He lived a life of humility and devotion to God. His Superior and the professors in the Seminary explained his poor performance and grades were the result of an inability to learn, and a lack of intelligence, *the more accurate explanation for Fr. Solanus' poor grades was that classes were taught in a foreign language, German.*

As a son of Irish immigrants, Father Solanus did not speak the German Language as did most of his fellow seminary students and teachers who were German immigrants.

In fact, he himself admitted he did so poorly because he had trouble learning German. But his life as a seminarian was extraordinarily holy and admirable. This was obvious to all!

When Fr. Solanus completed his studies as a seminarian, his superiors made the decision to have him ordained as a *"sacerdos simplex" (a simple priest)*. He accepted the decision with humility. As a young priest, he was not permitted to preach or hear confessions. Only a man of great faith in God's Will could submit himself as Fr. Solanus had in his life. Rather than follow his own desires, he took the difficult path of submitting his will with trust in God.

I imagine there are many people who have never seen an authentic healing of a serious condition or illness, such as a broken leg, a large tumor or cancer in its later stages disappearing from the body instantly and the person restored to good health. These actions are beyond Medical Science. Fr. Solanus Casey performed such healings as often as people came to him for help...which, of course, was daily.

Since our home was in the same neighborhood as St. Bonaventure Monastery, there were many stories by those healed or about those healed. I grew up in an atmosphere where healing was an accepted reality by my parents, relatives and any neighbors in the area.

When I was fifteen years old and a Voice told me I would see a healing in Carey, Ohio at the Shrine of Our Lady of Consolation, I did not doubt it. I was well aware of the hundreds of people God healed through Fr. Solanus. I actually expected to witness a healing at the Shrine. I was not really ready to have a special role in witnessing my first physical healing. When the healing did take place, I was an eye witness to the incredible Power of God at work.

I recall this miraculous healing very vividly...among the thousands of people present for the annual Feast day of Our Lady of Consolation -- the same day as August 15, celebrating the Assumption of the Mother of Jesus into Heaven -- there was a young lad about my age in a wheelchair who caught my attention since he had no feet! Below his knees his legs were completely deformed. I was watching him closely because I felt sure in my heart that he was the one chosen to be healed. At the proper time when the priest gave a Solemn Blessing on the crowd of more than 40,000 people, my eyes were glued to the *deformed twigs* at the end of his legs. At the very moment when the Blessing was given, the legs of the boy in the wheelchair started to move, twist and turn until there grew two beautiful feet right in front of my eyes! There were no feet a moment ago! Now he was able to step out of the wheelchair and walk for the first time in his life. At the age of fifteen, my conviction and Rite of Passage was beyond any doubt whatsoever that healing was definitely possible! It was an experience I shall never forget!

On other visits to the Shrine of Our Lady of Consolation, I saw two other healings. As a matter of fact, all through my priestly life, some healings took place when I blessed people, because I *knew* it was possible and they supplied a profound and trusting *Faith*.

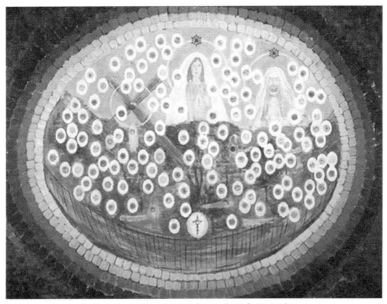

Mystical Vision by Rev. Jay Samonie

When I was only seven years old, I had another RITE OF PASSAGE. *I KNEW THERE WAS ANOTHER WORLD FAR GREATER AND MORE BEAUTIFUL THAN ANYTHING IN THIS WORLD.*

- 25 -

The vision I experienced with my brother and two of my sisters remains deeply in my memory and awareness...nearly seventy years later. The vision we shared for over an hour at Mt. Elliott Cemetery in Detroit is unforgettable, and if I were questioned, undeniable. I could also never forget the privilege of being an eye-witness to a vision of the Spirit World with countless souls descending from the heavens and countless others ascending.

Since that time, and at such a young age, I have always believed that death was not the end of life but rather a new beginning in the Spirit World. I have learned since that time, that Life in the Spirit World, which we call Heaven, there are many Levels or Realms of Light. It represents the next dimension for us on *Earth.* It is not a *place,* but rather *a state of mind* in which we continue to progress through unconditional Love, Forgiveness and Service to others. As we progress, we keep moving upward toward a higher Realm of Light and closer to our everlasting Home in God's Kingdom. (With the Knowledge I have today, the fact is that we never left God's Eternal Realm; we can't be separated from God even if we believe we are. More about that later!)

Sacred Heart Major Seminary, Detroit, Michigan

CHAPTER 3
CALLED TO BE A PRIEST

By the time I was 14 years old, I was being groomed for another leap in awareness. It was a very difficult spiritual

Rite of Passage for me. In the previous books I have published, I related how the Holy Spirit continually kept me on a certain path. The Holy Spirit even spoke to me verbally if I strayed from my spiritual path. It was as if I were engaged in an ordinary conversation with a friend. I am convinced that if someone else were present, two distinct voices would be heard: mine and the Holy Spirit! I was told out loud or verbally that my script in this lifetime was to enter the Catholic priesthood. *This Rite of Passage did not go well with me.* I firmly disagreed with the whole idea. I had other plans and even registered at another school; however, after having more than one discussion with God's Divine Messenger, I thought I had better apply to enter the Seminary. It was an important Rite of Passage for me to know that the Holy Spirit was alive and active in the world, but having the Holy Spirit personally guiding me to fulfill my destiny was, and still is, far beyond anything I could have imagined! I always had the same thought: Why me? (After being a Senior Priest over fifty years later, I was finally told why....but that is something I cannot share publicly!)

I took huge steps in spiritual development through many critical moments in the Seminary. I was only fourteen years old. My parents were a simple, religious, Lebanese-American family, whose culture was far different than that of an average American family. My father always spoke Arabic to me, our daily diet was Lebanese cooking, we all preferred listening to Middle East music for enjoyment and danced with an Arabic style of movement just as they still do today in Middle Eastern countries. I grew up with a deep faith, fostered by my parents and grandparents; nevertheless, outside our home and a secure family structure, I was a naive and somewhat shy young lad. I had a lot to learn.

In the Seminary, we had knowledgeable and competent Professors and I was a fairly good student, but when I reflect back on those days, I think I learned more about *Life Itself* through my classmates. We talked a lot, played sports together, had classes together and shared some happy as well as unhappy experiences with each other. It meant a lot to me that we sang daily together and prayed as a group.

HAVING GONE THROUGH FOUR YEARS OF HIGH SCHOOL, FOUR YEARS OF COLLEGE AND FOUR YEARS OF THEOLOGY IN THE SEMINARY, MY SPIRITUAL RITES OF PASSAGE WERE MANY. We had classes in basic subjects taught in every high school, but the Seminary College (equivalent to a University) and the Post Graduate Courses in Theology were much different. Since we were being trained at Sacred Heart Seminary in Detroit and at St. John's Major Seminary in Plymouth, Michigan to be Catholic Priests, our curriculum included Biblical and Sacramental Courses, such as Dogma, Moral Theology and Canon Law. Also, we were introduced to several major Philosophers and Theologians, the principal one being St. Thomas Aquinas who lived in the Thirteenth Century. Our Courses were based on his outstanding works. Some classes were taught in Latin, the universal language of the Catholic Church at that time. For certain classes, Latin was required of us just as German was for Fr. Solanus.

The Greek language was important too. I had five years of studies in Greek. It was important to have some basic knowledge in Greek since the New Testament of the Bible was written in Greek originally, except for the Gospel of St. Matthew which was written in Hebrew. At one point, the Old Testament of the Bible was translated by Jewish Scholars from Hebrew into pre-Christian Greek called the Septuagint.

Some people today, knowing very little Biblical History, still think the Bible was written in English and memorize word for word a mere translation of a text taken out of the Bible in English. It is very commendable if the English translation inspires people. There is nothing wrong with that, but they should also know that there are several different translations of the Scriptures, each one claiming to be the correct one. One thing is certain: The Bible was not written in English!

St. Jerome, was born in 340 A.D. in Dalmatia, a region of Yugoslavia on the Adriatic Sea. He was baptized a Catholic when he was eighteen years old. After living as a hermit in Palestine, St. Jerome went to Rome. Much against his will and with great humility, he was ordained a priest. St. Damasus, the thirty-ninth Pope, commissioned him to translate the whole Bible into Latin. It took St. Jerome fourteen years to make his first version of the Bible or Holy Scriptures in Latin, in what is known as the Latin Vulgate. A few more years were required to make corrections and then, in the beginning of the fifth century, the work was completed.

St. Jerome earned the right to be declared a Doctor of the Church. He died in Bethlehem in 420 A.D. English translations of the Bible came many centuries later. It is important to remember that Jesus never spoke in English. His native tongue was Aramaic, a Dialect of Hebrew. What we have in our English Bibles today are the various interpretations of Bible Scholars, making every effort to translate Aramaic into a current English language. Unfortunately, they do not all agree with each other. Nevertheless, and what is first and foremost, is not a translation on paper, even if it is called the Bible. What is important is not the translation itself, so much as establishing a personal relationship with the Lord Jesus.

What was life like in the Seminary? I can only say that no two days were alike. I grew from one Rite of Passage to another almost every day. In fact, when I look over my twelve years in the Seminary, the countless Rites of Passage changed me from a young, simple and innocent High School kid into a knowledgeable Philosopher and Theologian, ready to be ordained a priest and serve any parish and congregation to which I might be assigned.

I must confess that some Rites of Passage during my Seminary years did not come easy! Even after such Guidance from Above, I had to be reminded each year that I was called to be a priest in this lifetime, even though my heart was not in it. In fact, I decided to quit the Seminary every year. Yes! I am saying that for ten years in a row, I decided to leave the Seminary and go home, but the Messenger from Heaven convinced me each year verbally that it was my calling. I wanted to get married and have children like my parents and siblings did. My siblings (six sisters and one brother,) were certainly called to the married life. Although I never married, I do have a large family. I have 212 nieces and nephews as of this writing. Just taking care of their Baptisms and Marriages has been a busy sideline for me.

At first, I had no idea that my Lord and Master Jesus along with the Holy Spirit were guiding me through a path of experiences that would open my mind to some very surprising belief systems and philosophies.

THIS WAS A SURPRISING RITE OF PASSAGE: IT APPEARED THAT THROUGH DIVINE GUIDANCE I WAS SLOWLY BEING LEAD INTO THE KNOWLEDGE OF METAPHYSICS AND MYSTICISM.

It was inconceivable that I personally began to have some mystical and spiritual experiences that were nothing less than awesome...and exciting! I thought such experiences were reserved for people much greater than myself!

"Where was this going?" I asked myself.

"When does it stop? Will their Guidance end someday when I get older?"

Though I did not understand where my Divine Guides were leading me, I kept moving forward since my trust in them was one hundred percent!

I did feel a *transformation* in my previous views about life, death and purpose of being in a physical body at this time. Naturally, all my spiritual values began to change.

I never dreamed of pursuing any Academic Degrees beyond what we earned in the Seminary, but I became shocked at my own behavior when I pursued other fields of study until, years later, in 1988, I actually earned a Doctorate in Metaphysics. I also acquired two Master Degrees, one in Detroit and the other in Texas. Through the years, my pursuit and understanding of Truth has became much more realistic and profound.

I would like to state it as clearly as I can that my spiritual Rites of Passage were not an exception. My only advantage was that I was verbally and openly guided. I am sure that everyone has had experiences that shaped the underlying fabric and formation of their lives as well. We simply are not always aware of God's constant and perpetual action in the world...particularly in our own lives.

In fact, I have come to believe that all of us, without exception, have a script (or mission) to follow in our life here on earth. The script was written before we were born. We came here to remember who we are and to experience what is already known. Briefly stated, the Earth is one gigantic school with each of us coming here temporarily to learn some important lesson or lessons in our spiritual path by having certain experiences. No one else in the world has the same spiritual path as you do and God is ever at your side helping you to fulfill your pre-arranged personal script.

While we are in this third dimension, it is easy to get distracted from our original purpose and to forget that God, as Creator of all life, has a special interest in each one of us. Every person on this planet is important in the sight of Almighty God Who is the Divine Parent of every human being and the Source of all who share His Eternal Kingdom. Again, I say that there are no exceptions. You are one of God's infinite number of children, all siblings in God's One Creation or Extension of Himself, popularly known as the Son of God or the Christ.

Father Thomas Merton

CHAPTER 4
THOMAS MERTON

As a young ordained priest, my next Spiritual Rite of Passage came through Thomas Merton. (1915-1968) I was Pastor of

St. Michael's Church in Pontiac in the early seventies. I was awakened one night about 4:00 am. I opened my eyes and a man was standing at the foot of my bed. He was obviously from the Spirit World. I was not afraid. I simply asked who he was and why he was present. He never said a word then disappeared. I thought that was quite odd. I went back to sleep. The very next day, he was present again.

I said, "If you are going to remain silent again, this conversation is over!"

He did speak: "Don't you know who I am?"

I said: "No!"

"Does the name Thomas Merton sound familiar?", he replied. I had seen Thomas

Merton in person when I made a retreat at the Trappist Monastery in Louisville, Kentucky. He was on the other side of the street and with a hood over his face and wearing long flowing robes, he appeared to be tall and slender. The image standing in front of my bed was short and stocky. I was not convinced that the image I saw in my bedroom was really Thomas Merton.

Since I usually don't give up easily, I went to the Catholic Book Store in Downtown Detroit and asked for all of the books about Thomas Merton. One of the books had what I was looking for: *pictures* of Thomas Merton. It was a Pictorial Biography of him. I couldn't believe it! He really was short and stocky!

Thomas Merton is acclaimed as one of the most influential American spiritual writers of the twentieth century. His autobiography,

The Seven Storey Mountain, has sold over one million copies and has been translated into twenty-eight languages. Merton wrote over sixty other books and hundreds of poems and articles on topics ranging from monastic spirituality to civil rights, nonviolence, and the nuclear arms race.

During his last years, he became deeply interested in Asian religions, particularly Zen Buddhism, and in promoting East-West dialogue. After several meetings with Merton during the American monk's trip to the Far east in 1968, the Dalai Lama praised him as having a more profound understanding of Buddhism than any other Christian he had known. Actually, it was during a trip to a conference of the East-West Monastic Dialogue in Bangkok that Merton died. It was December 10, 1968, which by a sad coincidence, was the same date that marked his 27th anniversary of his entrance into the Trappist Monastery at Gethsemani, Kentucky.

Through Merton and his writings, I became vitally interested in the topics he wrote about, especially his outstanding poetry, civil rights, non-violence and the nuclear arms race. *I WAS ALSO ATTRACTED TO HIS APPRECIATION OF THE PHENOMENAL WISDOM OF GURUS AND OTHER RELIGIOUS TEACHERS FROM THE FAR EAST. FOR ME, AS AN AMERICAN, IT WAS A SPIRITUAL RITE OF PASSAGE.* I had to rethink my deepest convictions. Where did Hinduism, and the Far East Master-Teachers such as Buddha, Ramakrishna, Confucius and Paramahamsa Yogananda fit into the context of Reality?

Yet, some of the Far East and Asian Belief Systems that preceded Christianity by over 1,000 years are still current and their Scriptures are filled with wisdom. The most sacred scriptures of Hinduism are the Vedas ("Books of Knowledge"), a collection of texts written in Sanskrit from about 1200 BC. The Upanishads or Vedas are philosophical works that introduce the now-central ideas of self-realization, yoga, meditation and karma. The word "Upanishad" means "to sit down near," bringing to mind pupils gathering around their teacher for philosophical instruction. My awareness went far beyond the limitations of merely seeking only one path to Almighty God. There are many paths that lead to the same Source. So many different cultures on this planet have produced many different religious Belief Systems. One could hardly expect them all to agree on *one theology*.

It was time to move on to the knowledge and respect that every religion has to offer. Because someone worships God in a new and different manner does not mean that they are wrong. As a matter fact, the last two Popes, John Paul II and Benedict XVI have both shown great respect toward the Jews, the Muslims, the Anglicans and other Christian and non-Christian Belief Systems. No single religion has a monopoly on Absolute Truth. In this world in which we have an extremely limited knowledge of the Universe, that would be a perfect example of *arrogance*! Knowing Infinite and Absolute Truth is reserved to the Creator alone, although Almighty God occasionally offers us a glimpse of His Eternal Kingdom. We, as Christians, have received a small portion of the Total Truth through Our Lord Jesus Christ.

It is so depressing to me that the homeland of my Lebanese parents and ancestors is used as a battleground between certain people who have been enemies for centuries. I pray every day that they would forgive one another, since all is One. We all belong to the same Family of God, although Almighty God is known by different names.

On my last visit to Israel, which was one of the lands we visited during a cruise in the Mediterranean Sea, I was asked by several people on the cruise why the Arabs and the Jews disliked each other so much. I did not have much to say at that time. However, in the process of obtaining a Master's Degree in Biblical Theology, I discovered something very interesting.

I do not intend the following statement to be political by any means, but as a scripture scholar, the Bible offers some light on the Middle East situation.

In the very first Book of the Old Testament, the story of Abraham unfolds in Genesis 16:

> Abram's wife Sarai (before God had renamed both of them: Abraham and Sarah) had borne him no children. She had, however, an Egyptian maidservant named Hagar. Sarai said to Abram: The Lord has kept me from having children. "Have relations with my maid; perhaps I shall have sons through her." Hagar became pregnant and looked on her mistress with disdain...Sarai responded by verbally abusing her to such a degree that Hagar decided to run away from her.
>
> The Lord's messenger told Hagar (as she was traveling from that area), "Go back to your mistress...I will make your descendants so numerous," added the messenger, "that they will

be too numerous to count." Then the Lord's messenger said to her:

"You are now pregnant and shall bear a son; you shall name him Ishmael; for the Lord has heard you, God had answered you."

In his old age of 86, Abraham was told he would have a son by Sarah who was also in her old age. They did not think it possible, so Sarah laughed when told this, but the Lord's words were true. She bore a son and called him Isaac, meaning "she laughed!"

Concerning Isaac, "God said I will keep my covenant with him as an everlasting pact, to be his God and the God of his descendants after him. (This was the origin of the Jewish nation.) As for Ishmael I hereby bless him. I will make him fertile and will multiply him exceedingly. He shall become the father of twelve chieftains and I will make of him a great nation." (This was the origin of the Arab nations.)

The question comes up: just who is this Abraham, the father and founder of both the Jewish and Arab nations?

According to the Bible, the Book of Genesis gives the genealogy of Abraham, going back in time, to Seth, the son of Adam. Abraham was living in the city of Ur in Babylonia, (located today in Southern Iraq) when God sent him forth on his wanderings to the land of Canaan. Abraham was called an "elect of God" (some translations called him "mighty prince" in Chapter 23 of Genesis.) Later generations referred to the God of Abraham called Yahweh (or Jehovah).

From this one man emerged one single family whose relatives now oppose each other: the Arabs and the Jews. Both the Jews and the Arab people claim Abraham as their ancestral father and they are both correct! And both have God's blessing. Unfortunately, through the mothers of Isaac (a Jew) and Ishmael (an Arab) the two boys grew up at odds with each other and their descendants still are. They all came from the same family tree and are related as distant cousins.

Father Pierre Teilhard De Chardin

CHAPTER 5
TEILHARD DE CHARDIN

I am well aware of my spiritual Rite of
Passage just knowing about Teilhard de
Chardin. I learned a lot through his life and

works. Pierre Teilhard de Chardin lived from May 1, 1881 to April 10, 1955. He was a Jesuit priest, an original-thinking philosopher, a theologian and also a trained paleontologist.

Teilhard was, more then anything else, a relentless researcher. He was one of the first to propose a synthesis of the History of the Universe as it is generally explained by present-day scientists. The vision he puts forward in his different writings, particularly in "The Phenomenon of Man", is hinged on *evolution*. His outstanding concepts include the theory that the earth is enveloped in a layer of thought, which he calls the "noosphere", and his explanation of the planetisation (He often had to make up new words to explain his theories) phenomenon with which we are faced today.

In setting forth this sweeping account of the unfolding of the material cosmos, he abandoned the literal interpretation of the creation account in the first Book of the Bible, called Genesis (that the creation of the world was only about 4 thousand years ago) in favor of a metaphorical interpretation. In so doing, he displeased the ultra-conservative Cardinal Ottaviani, a member of the Roman Curia in the Vatican. Ottaviani considered Teilhard's teaching an undermining of the Catholic doctrine of original sin. Teilhard's work was considered controversial and therefore denied publication while Teilhard was still living.

Teilhard was sent to China to be as far away as possible. The Church authorities believed that people would soon forget him and his wild theories! On the contrary, it was ironic and almost laughable that when

Teilhard was sent to China, they sent him to the very place where he easily proved his point.

He happened to be present near Beijing at the Zhoukoudian Peking Man Site where fissures in the limestone containing middle Pleistocene deposits yielded the remains of about 40 individuals as well as animal remains, layers of stone and chopping tools. The oldest are some 500,000 years old. That was clear scientific evidence that in The Peking Man findings, there was ample scientific proof that human beings lived at least 500,000 years ago. (At the present time, the Scientific Community have positive evidence that human beings lived on Earth over four million years ago!)

He conceived such ideas as the Omega Point and the Noosphere. (One of my paintings is called Omega *Point*. I had him in mind when I painted it.)

However, many years later, when the Vatican II Council took place in 1963, Teilhard was once again held in high esteem in the Catholic Church. He just happened to be ahead of his time! No one in their right mind today believes that the earth was created only four thousand years ago. There is ample and absolute proof to the contrary in today's world.

Speaking of his belief in Divine Guidance, Teilhard declared to the Heavens: "If, in my life, I have *not* been wrong, I beg God to allow me to die on Easter Sunday". April 10, 1955, was Easter Sunday. On that very day, he died shortly after celebrating Mass.

REGARDLESS OF WHAT IS BEING TAUGHT OUT THERE IN THE WORLD, DIVINE GUIDANCE IS SUPERIOR TO HUMAN KNOWLEDGE AND SHOULD BE FOLLOWED. THIS WAS ANOTHER RITE OF PASSAGE FOR ME. The Lord has been openly guiding me all my life. I have heard, witnessed and experienced Divine Guidance and wrote about it in all the books I have authored. The works of great minds like Teilhard de Chardin affirmed that following Divine Guidance will ultimately be accepted as Truth...at some point in time.

Teilhard's concept of a noosphere surrounding the earth and made up of the thoughts of human beings is similar to Carl Jung's *Universal Archetypes* found in the mind and heart of every human being. One major archetype is a *Madonna* painting by one of the Master Artists. She holds her child close to her breast...the universal symbol, of course, being *UNCONDITIONAL LOVE. THIS WAS ANOTHER RITE OF PASSAGE,* which had a deep impact on my sense of awareness and spiritual development.

St. Teresa Of Avila

CHAPTER 6
ST. TERESA OF ÁVILA

Many people think that centuries ago
women were not educated or allowed to
make contributions to the Church or to

Society in general. The story of St. Teresa of Ávila, St. Catherine of Sienna, St. Hildegarde and other great women prove that this was not the case. Their knowledge and teachings were held in the highest regard by Popes, Statesmen and Kings.

I was particularly interested in the life of St. Teresa of Ávila. She was born in Spain and she loved to read, especially stories about saints. When she was twelve and nearly grown up for those times, her mother died. Her father decided that the best place for Teresa to live was in the Augustinian Convent. Teresa liked living with the nuns in the convent; it was a happy and peaceful place. She saw that joining a convent was a good way to serve God and grow closer to Him. However, when it was time for her to leave the Augustinians and return home to her father, she had already decided to become a *Carmelite* nun rather than an *Augustinian* nun.

She made her profession at the Carmelite Convent of the Incarnation when she was 19 years old. This, of course, is not the end of the story. Teresa was disappointed that being a nun was not as easy and as peaceful as she had expected. She found it hard to pray. There were many distractions. Even when she tried, she found it hard to concentrate. Since she liked having friends and being among people, it was difficult to spend time in prayer.

Finally, after many trials and years of trying, Teresa received the grace she prayed for. God became her best Friend. She wanted to spend all her time with Him and found the peace and happiness she had been looking for all her life. Inspired by the

Holy Spirit and her new friendship with God, she began to reform the Carmelite Religious Order. At that time, the Carmelite's allowed women other than nuns to live in the convent. These women had parties and visitors; they didn't work or pray, or try to live a life of poverty.

Teresa knew that this made it hard for the nuns to concentrate and pray, so she started to reorganize the Religious Order. She founded several new Convents all over Europe that followed a stricter, simpler rule. She wrote letters to her Sisters, and books about prayer and spiritual life that the Popes of the time considered to be great additions to the knowledge and tradition of the Church. Her *"Autobiography", "The Way of Perfection,"* and the *"The Interior Castle"*, form a collection so remarkable with which only the "*Confessions of St. Augustine*" can bear comparison.

On the eve of the festival of the Most Holy Trinity, Teresa was praying about a subject she should choose for this treatise, when God, Who disposes all things in due form and order, granted her request and provided a subject. He showed her a most beautiful crystal globe, made in the shape of a castle (the origin of the Interior Castle) containing seven mansions. In the seventh and innermost of which was the King of Glory, in the greatest splendor, illumining and beautifying them all. The nearer one got to the center, the stronger was the light; outside the palace limits everything was foul, dark and infested with toads, vipers and other venomous creatures.

Here, in detail, are the seven Mansions inspired by Divine Guidance:

FIRST MANSIONS. This chapter begins with a meditation on the excellence and dignity of the human soul, made as it is in the image and likeness of God: the author laments that more pains are not taken by each soul to perfect it. The souls in the First Mansions are in a state of grace, but are still very much in love with the venomous creatures outside the castle and need a long and searching discipline before they can make any progress. So they stay for a long time in the Mansions of Humility, in which, since the heat and light from within reach them only in a faint and diffused form, all is cold and dim.

SECOND MANSIONS. But all the time the soul is anxious to penetrate farther into the castle, so it seeks every opportunity of advancement -- sermons, edifying conversations, good company and so on. It is doing its utmost to put its desires into practice: these are the Mansions of the Practice of Prayer. It is not yet completely secure from the attacks of the poisonous reptiles which infest the courtyard of the castle but its powers of resistance are increasing. There is more warmth and light here than in the First Mansions.

THIRD MANSIONS. The description of these Mansions of Exemplary Life begins with stern exhortations on the dangers of trusting to one's own strength and to the virtues one has already acquired, which must still of necessity be very weak. Yet, although the soul which reaches the Third Mansions may still fall back, it has attained a high standard of virtue. Controlled by discipline and penance and disposed to performing acts of charity toward others, it has acquired prudence and discretion and orders its life well. Its limitations are those of vision: it has not yet experienced the full and inspiring force of love. It has not made a full and total self-surrender. Its love is still governed by reason, so its progress is slow. It suffers from aridity and is given only occasional glimpses into the Mansions beyond.

FOURTH MANSIONS. Here the supernatural element of the mystical life first enters: that is to say, it is no longer by its own efforts that the soul is acquiring what it gains. Henceforward, the soul's part will become increasingly less and God's part increasingly greater. The graces of the Fourth Mansions, referred to as "spiritual consolations", are identified with the Prayer of Quiet in Life. The soul is like a fountain built near its source and the water of life flows into it, not through an aqueduct, but directly from the spring. Its love is now free from servile fear: it has broken all the bonds which previously hindered its progress; it shrinks from no trials and attaches no importance to anything to do with the world. It can pass rapidly from ordinary to inspired prayer and back again. It has not yet, however, received the highest gifts of the Spirit and relapses are still possible.

FIFTH MANSIONS. This is the state described elsewhere the Spiritual Betrothal and the Prayer of Union -- that is, the early stages of inspired Union with God. It marks a new degree of contemplation. By means of the most celebrated of all her metaphors, that of the silkworm, St. Teresa explains how far the soul can prepare itself to receive what is essentially a gift from God. She also describes the psychological conditions of this state, in which, for the first time, the faculties of the soul are "asleep". It is of short duration, but while it lasts, the soul is completely possessed by God.

SIXTH MANSIONS. In the Fifth Mansions, the soul is, as it were, betrothed to its future Spouse. In the Sixth, Lover and Beloved see each other for long periods at a time and as they grow in intimacy, the soul receives increasing favors together with increasing afflictions. The afflictions, which give the description of these Mansions and their characteristic colors are dealt with in some detail. They may be purely exterior bodily sickness: misrepresentation, backbiting, persecution or undeserved praise. Or they may come partly or wholly from within -- and the depression which can afflict the soul in the Sixth Mansions, says St. Teresa, is comparable only with the tortures of hell. Yet it has no desire to be freed from them except by entering the innermost Mansions of all.

SEVENTH MANSIONS. Here at last the soul reaches the Spiritual Marriage. Here dwells the King -- "it may be called another Heaven": the two lighted candles join and become one, the falling rain becomes merged in the river. There is complete transformation, ineffable and perfect peace; no higher state is conceivable, save that of the Beatific Vision (seeing God face to face) in the life to come.

While each of these seven Mansions is described with the greatest possible clarity, St. Teresa makes it quite plain that she does not regard her description as excluding others. Each of the series of mansions (called moradas in Spanish) using the *plural* throughout, especially in the title of each chapter), is noteworthy and may contain as many as a million rooms; all matters connected with spiritual progress are susceptible to numerous interpretations, for the grace of God knows no limit or measure.

Her description is based largely on her own experience; and, though this has been found to correspond very nearly with that of most other great mystics, there are various divergences on points of detail. She never for a moment intended her path to be followed step by step and she frequently reminds us of this.

At the end of this last, most mystical and most mature of her books, St. Teresa invites all her daughters to enter the Interior Castle, drawing a picturesque contrast between the material poverty of the convents of the

Reform and the spiritual luxury and beauty of the Mansions -- where, as she delightfully puts it, they can go as often as they please without needing to ask the permission of their Superiors. There is no doubt whatever that she considered mystical experience to be within the reach of all her daughters. This conviction is repeated so frequently in the Way of Perfection and in the Interior Castle that it needs no particular references. She does not, of course, mean that every one of her nuns who prepares herself as far as she can to receive mystical favors does, in fact, receive them. She could not presume to pronounce upon the secret judgments of God. But, she evidently believes that generally speaking, infused contemplation is accessible to any Christian who has the resolution to do all that is in him towards obtaining it.

This journey is more clearly seen, perhaps, through the vision of the soul given to St. Teresa in the "Interior Castle." In the seven Mansions Teresa saw seven dwellings of the soul, toward its end — the Holy Trinity. While cautioning against a simplistic reading or thoughts of a linear progression as though step 1 leads next to step 2, etc., Teresa insisted that "You mustn't think of these dwelling places in such a way that each one would follow in file one after the other, but turn your eyes toward the center, which is the room or royal chamber where the King stays. Hence, the "first mansions" are all those rooms most distant from the center and from the King, who dwells in that center.

Her Feast day is October 15. St. Teresa was canonized in 1662 by Pope Gregory XV and was declared a Doctor of the Church, the first woman so honored, in 1970 by Pope Paul VI.

She died after having a vision of Jesus and many Saints waiting to welcome her to her heavenly Home.

Teresa's extraordinary love for God, having spiritual and mystical experiences and being guided by the Holy Spirit was an inspiration to me. *THROUGH ST. TERESA, MY SPIRITUAL RITE OF PASSAGE WAS A STRONGER AND MORE PROFOUND ATTRACTION TO MYSTICISM AND DIVINE GUIDANCE.* My own experiences were also confirmed.

St. John of the Cross

CHAPTER 7
ST. JOHN OF THE CROSS

One of the most important mystical philosophers in Christian History was St. John of the Cross. The son of a rich merchant,

John was born Juan de Yepes y Alvarez in Fontiveros, Spain in 1542. John's father died when he was quite young, leaving his mother, a member of a lower social class, to raise him alone. After gaining employment in a hospital, John, at age 18 began to study with the Jesuits. He later entered the Carmelite Order in 1563, continuing his studies at the University of Salamanca, where he began to teach while still a student. After being ordained in 1567, John met St. Teresa of Ávila.

As a child he lived in various Castilian villages, the last being Medina del Campo, where he moved in 1551. There, he studied the humanities at a Jesuit school from 1559 to 1563 and then entered the Carmelite Order, adopting the name Fr. Juan de Santo Matía.

The following year (1564) he was professed as a Carmelite and moved to Salamanca, where he studied at the University and at the College of St. Andrew. This experience would influence all his later writings, as Fr. Luis de León taught Biblical Studies (Exegesis, Hebrew and Aramaic) at the University. León was one of the foremost experts in Biblical Studies and had written an important and controversial translation of the Song of Songs into Spanish. (Translation of the Bible into the vernacular was not allowed then in Spain).

Following Teresa's lead in attempting to reform his Religious Order, John, in 1568, initiated a very severe form of monasticism in a tiny farmhouse. These monks went so far as to go barefoot, indicating their commitment to poverty, and so they were called: "discalced" or "shoeless." Over time, a rift arose between the traditional Carmelites and John's Discalced Carmelites, leading in 1576 to John's arrest and imprisonment.

In 1575 at Piacenza in Italy, the Carmelite Religious Order suppressed those monasteries of the Reform which had been founded without the authorization of the Superior General of the Monastery. Nothing was done to put this decree into effect, however, as long as Ormaneto, the Papal Nuncio, who was friendly to the Reform, was in office. After his death, however, and with the coming of Sega, also a Papal Nuncio from the Vatican but hostile to the Reform, the Calced Carmelites followed an easier and more comfortable Observance. They were even able to call on the Civil arm of the Law and had a number of the *Reformed Discalced Fathers* arrested.

St. John of the Cross was taken prisoner on December 3, 1577 from his chaplain's house at the Convent of the Incarnation in Ávila and brought to Toledo. He immediately became aware that the decrees of Piacenza, which were read to him, referred only to houses founded without the Prior General's permission.

But St. John would not renounce the Reform, as he was called on to do. Therefore, he was termed rebellious and contumacious and was imprisoned in a Toledo Monastery in a room ten feet by six, with a very small slit high in the wall being his only source of light.

The key to the trouble was a conflict of power and authority between the Prior General of the Carmelite Order and the Papal Nuncio in Spain.

The room was really nothing but a large closet. Here St. John was locked in for nine months, suffering from the cold in the winter and the stifling heat in the summer. When he was brought out, it was to take his meal of bread and water and sometimes sardines, kneeling in the refectory and to hear the repeated, violent scoldings of the Prior. After the meal on Fridays, he had to bare his shoulders and undergo the *circular discipline* for the space of a certain prayer. Each person present struck him in turn with a lash. St. John bore the scars of those beatings throughout the rest of his life.

There were other cruelties leading to a complete crushing of the Reform. All the letters of St. Teresa of Avila to the King of Spain, Philip II and others were to no avail. No one even knew where John was kept. "I do not know how it comes about that there is never anyone who remembers this holy man," St. Teresa complained in one letter.

In the darkness of this cell, St. John of the Cross composed and committed to memory some of his greatest poems, including most of his book, "The Spiritual Canticle", which is 40 stanzas in length. On August 14, when the Prior, the stern Fray Maldonaldo, came to St. John's cell and asked what he was thinking about since he did not rise, St. John replied, "That tomorrow is Our Lady's Feast and how much I should love to say Mass."

"Not while I am here," the Prior replied.

On August 15, 1578, St. John escaped at night from the Toledo Monastery by improvising a rope knotting together with his sheets. Unfortunately, the rope did not reach far enough so he had to jump down onto the ramparts, narrowly missing the chasm of rocks by the banks of the Tajo where he would have been dashed to pieces. His sufferings and spiritual endeavors were reflected in all of his subsequent writings.

Later, after his incarceration was over, St. John of the Cross never said a word against those who had treated him so badly. "They did it because they did not understand," he said in excuse. He bore no ill-feeling toward his "jailers," for his soul was unruffled and at peace and dwelt with God.

After returning to his normal life, he went on with the reformation and the founding of monasteries until his death on December 14, 1591.

His writings were first published in 1618. He was canonized a Saint by Benedict XIII in 1726. In 1926, he was declared a Doctor of the Church by Pope Pius XI. The Church of England commemorates him as a "Teacher of the Faith", celebrating his Feast Day on December 14.

St. John of the Cross is considered one of the foremost poets in the Spanish language, composing approximately 2500 verses. Two of them: "The Spiritual Canticle" and "The Dark Night of the Soul" are widely considered to be among the best poems ever written in Spanish, both for their formal stylistic point of view and their rich symbolism and imagery.

The Spiritual Canticle is a pastoral poem or *eclogue* in which the bride (representing the soul) searches for the bridegroom (representing Jesus Christ) and is anxious at having lost him; both are filled with joy upon reuniting. It can be seen as a free-form Spanish version of the Song of songs at a time when translations of the Bible into vernacular were forbidden!

"The Dark Night of the Soul" (from which the popular term Dark Night of the Soul takes its name) narrates the journey of the soul from her bodily home to her union with God. It happens during the night, which represents the hardships and difficulties she meets in detachment from the world and reaching the light of the union with the Creator. There are several steps in this night, which are related in successive stanzas.

St. John also wrote three treatises on Mystical Theology, two of them concerning the two poems above, and supposedly explaining the meaning of the poems verse by verse and even word by word. He actually proves unable to follow this scheme and writes freely on the subject he is treating at each time. The third work, "Ascent of Mount Carmel" is a more systematic study of the ascetical endeavor of a soul looking for perfect union with God and the mystical events happening along the way. These, together with his "Sayings of Love and Peace" and St. Teresa's writings, are the most important mystical works in Spanish and have deeply influenced later spiritual writers all around the world. Among these can be named T. S. Eliot, Thérèse de Lisieux, Edith Stein (Teresa Benedicta of the Cross) and Thomas Merton. John has also influenced philosophers (Jacques Maritain), theologians (Hans Urs von Balthasar), and pacifists (Dorothy Day, Daniel Berrigan and Philip Berrigan).

During his period of imprisonment, John wrote much of the poetry that would provide his greatest contribution to later generations. Eventually, the rights of the Discalced Carmelites were completely acceptable and John took on various roles of leadership within the Religious Order. After some fifteen years of leadership, he died in 1591, leaving behind a number of remarkable works of Christian mysticism: *"Ascent of Mount Carmel"*, *"The Dark Night of the Soul"* and *"The Spiritual Canticle of the Soul."*

His famous work *"The Dark Night of the Soul"* inspired me deeply. *READING IT IN THE ORIGINAL SPANISH I WAS SO MOVED THAT IT BROUGHT TEARS TO MY EYES, AND WHILE MEDITATING ON THE POWERFUL MEANING OF HIS WORDS, MY SOUL FELT MOVED AND STRENGTHENED WITH AN UNSHAKEABLE*

CONVICTION AND ENLIGHTENMENT. THE
EFFECT ON ME WAS A HUGE RITE OF
PASSAGE.

Mayan

CHAPTER 8
A MAYAN ARCHITECT?

The next Rite of Passage was very powerful and life-changing. I was completely overwhelmed through a personal experience while on a Tour in Mexico. The Tour Bus to the pyramids was full and I did not know any other tourists, but amid total strangers the most extraordinary thing happened.

When we stopped at the famous Sun Pyramid next to Mexico City, we were given time to look around. I was about to be completely overwhelmed through a personal experience of another lifetime. It came about in the strangest way! While on this Tour, I was simply looking around when a lady from the bus asked if I would stand in front of the Sun Pyramid for a photo to give her folks back home an idea of just how large it is. It compared to the pyramids of Egypt in size! However, as soon as I saw the flash of light from her camera, an unforgettable experience took place immediately. I was suddenly transported back in time! I was wearing a loin cloth and sandals and nothing else. I began speaking the Mayan language; apparently, I had the experience of being a Mayan architect supervising a series of structures that joined the Sun Pyramid to the Moon Pyramid. They kept asking me questions about structural problems that only an architect could resolve.

There was nothing but a mile of desert that separated the two pyramids in 1955, the year of my visit, but, as a Mayan, we were building structures that joined the two pyramids. They would eventually be covered with sand and no longer visible. I was speaking the Mayan language as fluently as though it were my mother tongue but I also understood and spoke the language of the Teotihuacán Indians, who actually built the pyramids. I was merely brought in as an architect. I was wide awake and I still recall the whole experience very clearly.

The tour guide noticed I was not there when the bus was about to leave. He sent the same lady who took my picture and her friend to the spot where she last saw me. When they found me, I was still standing there...except for one thing: I was in a deep trance or rapture. I had no previous knowledge of what that meant. They couldn't awaken me right away! They told me afterwards that they kept slapping me and pinching me until I was awake! They eventually brought me back to the year 1955. I was still speaking the Mayan language when they awakened me from the trance. It took me a few moments before I realized I was no longer a Mayan architect. I was Jay Samonie and, after a pause, I began speaking English.

THIS RITE OF PASSAGE MADE ME DO A LOT OF THINKING ABOUT LIFE IN GENERAL. IS THERE SUCH A THING AS DÉJÀ VU OR REBIRTH? Just thinking seriously about such a subject raised my awareness immensely. I can't prove anything and I am not trying to, but I was speaking two languages fluently that I had never spoken before in this life. It never even remotely occurred to me that I would be speaking the Mayan and Teotihuacán languages. I was still only a young seminarian studying to be a priest.

Jesus' words in the Bible began to throw some light on my state of confusion. After all, three different times, Jesus said that John the Baptist was Elijah the great prophet of the Old Testament. How to interpret Jesus' words correctly, I do not know! Yet, the possibility of being reborn is certainly implied if it is not a fact and it is apparently not in conflict with the Christian belief that our souls are immortal while our physical bodies definitely are not.

I am simply relating my spiritual Rites of Passage and so I put the concept of Rebirth aside for awhile. What I experienced happened without the slightest doubt in my mind! Still, it was outside of and too progressive for the limited knowledge of a young Catholic seminarian in the year of 1955.

Diego Velasquiez

CHAPTER 9
DIEGO VELASQUEZ

This Rite of Passage added some weight to what I experienced at the Pyramids in Mexico. I was told by two different psychics (who did not know each other or had never seen me before) that I was the artist Diego Velasquez in a former life. I laughed both times telling them I did not believe in such nonsense. Two years later, I went to Spain and visited the famous Prado Museum in Madrid. After taking a tour of the Museum, my traveling buddy, Tom Bissonnette, and I happened to enter a big room with one large painting. As soon as I saw it I went into a trance or enraptured state (or whatever it is called) and I was actually painting that picture. Apparently, somebody passing by happened to bump against me and knocked me down. Tom turned around saw me on the floor. I must have looked ridiculous! When he helped me get on my feet, I was explaining to him that I was painting that picture. He asked who painted it? I didn't have any idea! Only when we walked up close to the painting on the wall did we discover that it was a painting by Diego Velasquez.

Again, I am not trying to *establish a universal truth. These were my actual, personal experiences* and the spiritual Rites of Passage were taking shape in *my thinking and in my convictions.* As a result of the experiences above, my mind was becoming open to my next spiritual Rite of Passage: *I CANNOT HELP BUT BELIEVE IN THE POSSIBILITY THAT WE MAY HAVE LIVED BEFORE, SINCE OUR SOULS ARE IMMORTAL.* On the other hand, I would never affirm that it was an absolute Truth since the subject of Rebirth is a larger than life mystery, yet to be resolved. My conclusions are simply based on a reliable teacher called *personal experience.* I am only relating my personal and spiritual Rites of Passage. The possibility of actually being a professional artist of the sixteenth century was an enlightening experience for me. Again, such theories did not fit into my theology or philosophy...for me, it was simply another Rite of Passage. I am sure that each of us has had at least one experience that would be hard to explain to another person.

Naturally, I became curious! Just who was Diego Velásquez? I read that he was born in 1599 and died in 1660. One of his biographies was written by Nicholas Pioch of the famous Paris Webmuseum. This ever-expanding Webmuseum Network is now welcoming 200,000 visitors every week, delivering over 10 million documents. The critic Nicholas Pioch considers Velasquez as Spain's greatest painter and was one of the supreme artists of all time. A master of technique and highly individual in style, Diego Velasquez may have had a greater influence on European art than any other painter.

Diego Rodriguez de Silva Velasquez was born in Seville, Spain. His father was of noble Portuguese descent. In his teens, he studied art with Francisco Pacheco, whose daughter he married. The young Velasquez once declared, "I would rather be the first painter of common things than second in higher art." He learned much from studying nature. After his marriage at the age of 19, Velasquez went to Madrid, where at 24, he painted a portrait of King Philip IV, who became his patron.

The artist made two visits to Italy. On his first, in 1629, he copied masterpieces in Venice and Rome. He returned to Italy 20 years later and brought many paintings by

Titian, Tintoretto, and Paolo Veronese and also a statuary for the King's Collection.

Except for these journeys, Velasquez lived in Madrid as a Court painter. His paintings include landscapes, mythological and religious subjects and scenes from common life, called genre pictures. Most of them, however, are portraits of court notables that rank with the portraits painted by Titian and Anthony Van Dyck.

Duties of Velasquez' royal offices also occupied his time. He was eventually made Marshal of the royal household, and as such he was responsible for the royal quarters and for planning ceremonies.

Velasquez had charge of his last and greatest ceremony —– the wedding of Maria Theresa to Louis XIV of France. This was a most elaborate affair. Worn out from these labors, Velasquez contracted a fever from which he died on August 6, 1660.

Velasquez was called the "noblest and most commanding man among the artists of his country." He was a master realist and no painter has surpassed him in the ability to seize essential features and fix them on canvas with a few broad, sure strokes. "His men and women seem to breathe," it has been said; "his horses are full of action and his dogs full of life."

Because of Velasquez' great skill in merging color, light, space, rhythm of line and mass in such a way that all have equal value, he was known as "the painter's painter." Ever since he taught Bartolomé Murillo, Velasquez has directly or indirectly led painters to make original contributions to the development of art. Others who have been noticeably influenced by him are Francisco de Goya, Camille Corot, Gustave Courbet, Edouard Manet and James McNeill Whistler. His famous paintings include *The Surrender of Breda*, An equestrian *portrait of Philip IV*, *The Spinners*, *The Maids of Honor*, *Pope Innocent X*, *Christ at Emmaus* and a portrait of the *Infanta Maria Theresa.*

I do not consider myself a great artist, although it is curious that, without any lessons or training in the art of painting, I have produced nearly 600 paintings in my lifetime and I have had three successful Art Exhibits in which all my paintings were sold. Could there possibly be a connection with Velasquez and my present lifetime? Did I somehow tap into his talent? I really do not know, but it is certainly an interesting concept.

Mother Teresa of Calcutta

CHAPTER 10
MOTHER TERESA

Another spiritual Rite of Passage was meeting Mother Teresa in person on two different occasions. She once said of herself, "By blood, I am Albanian. By citizenship, an Indian. By faith, I am a Catholic nun. As to my calling, I belong to the world. As to my heart, I belong entirely to the Heart of Jesus."

Small of stature, rocklike in faith, Mother Teresa of Calcutta was entrusted with the mission of proclaiming God's thirsting Love for humanity, especially for the poorest of the poor. She also said, "God still loves the world and He sends you and me to be His Love and His Compassion to the poor."

This outstanding messenger of God's love was born on August 26, 1910, in Skopje, a city situated at the crossroads of Balkan History. The youngest of the children born to Nikola and Drane Bojaxhiu, she was baptized Gonxha Agnes. From the day of her First Holy Communion, a love for souls was within her.

Her father's sudden death when young Gonxha (Teresa) was about eight years old left the family in dire financial straits. Drane raised her children firmly and lovingly, greatly influencing her daughter's character and vocation. Gonxha's religious formation was further assisted by the vibrant Jesuit Parish of the Sacred Heart, in which she was much involved.

At the age of eighteen, moved by a desire to become a missionary, Gonxha left her home in September 1928 to join the Institute of the Blessed Virgin Mary, known as the Sisters of Loreto, in Ireland. There she received the name Sister Mary Teresa after St. Thérèse of Lisieux.

In December, she departed for India, arriving in Calcutta on January 6, 1929. After making her First Profession of Vows in

May 1931, Sister Teresa was assigned to the Loreto Religious Community in Calcutta and taught at St. Mary's School for girls. On May 24, 1937, Sister Teresa made her Final Profession of Vows, becoming, as she said, the "spouse of Jesus for all eternity." From that time on she was called Mother Teresa. She continued teaching at St. Mary's and in 1944 became the school's Principal. A person of profound prayer and deep love for her Religious Sisters and her students, Mother Teresa's twenty years in Loreto were filled with profound happiness. Noted for her charity, unselfishness and courage, her capacity for hard work and a natural talent for organization, she lived out her consecration to Jesus, in the midst of her companions, with fidelity and joy.

On September 10, 1946, during the train ride from Calcutta to Darjeeling for her annual retreat, Mother Teresa received what she says was her *"inspiration"* or her *"call within a call."* On that day, in a way she never did explain, Jesus' thirst for Love and for souls took hold of her heart and the desire to satiate His thirst became the driving force of her life. Over the course of the next several months, by means of interior encounters and visions, Jesus revealed to her the desire of His heart for "victims of love who would radiate His Love for souls."

In my own life, I have also experienced visions of my Master and Teacher, Jesus. *KNOWING THAT MOTHER TERESA ALSO HAD SUCH ENCOUNTERS, SPIRITUALLY LIFTED MY SOUL TO ANOTHER RITE OF PASSAGE: SHE REINFORCED MY OWN BELIEF IN DIRECT COMMUNICATION WITH GOD'S FAVORED SON.*

"Come, be My light," Jesus begged her. "I cannot go alone." He revealed His pain at the neglect of the poor, His sorrow at their ignorance of Him and His longing for their Love. He asked Mother Teresa to establish the *Missionaries of Charity*, a Religious Community dedicated to serve the poorest of the poor. Nearly two years of testing and discernment passed before Mother Teresa received permission to begin. On August 17, 1948, she dressed for the first time in a white, blue-bordered sari to enter the world of the poor.

After a short Seminar with the Medical Mission Sisters in Patna, Mother Teresa returned to Calcutta and found temporary lodging with the Little Sisters of the Poor. On December 21, she went for the first time to the slums. She visited families, washed the sores of some children, cared for an old man lying sick on the road and nursed a woman dying of hunger and TB. She started each day in Communion with Jesus and then went out, rosary in her hand, to find and serve Him in "the unwanted, the unloved, the uncared for." After some months, she was joined, one by one, by her former students.

On October 7, 1950, the new Congregation of the Missionaries of Charity was officially established in the Archdiocese of Calcutta. By the early 1960s, Mother Teresa began to send her Sisters to other parts of India. The Decree of Praise granted to the Congregation by Pope Paul VI in February of 1965 encouraged her to open another Convent or Foundation in Venezuela. It was soon followed by Foundations in Rome, Tanzania and eventually, on every continent. Starting in 1980 and continuing through the 1990s,

Mother Teresa opened Convents in almost all of the Communist countries, including the former Soviet Union, Albania and Cuba.

In order to respond better to both the physical and spiritual needs of the poor, Mother Teresa founded the Missionaries of Charity in 1963, the contemplative branch of the Sisters in 1976, the Contemplative Brothers in 1979 and the Missionaries of Charity Fathers in 1984. Yet her inspiration was not limited to those with religious vocations. She formed the Co-Workers of Mother Teresa and the Sick and Suffering Co-Workers, people of many faiths and nationalities with whom she shared her spirit of prayer, simplicity, sacrifice and her apostolate of humble works of love. This spirit later inspired the Lay Missionaries of Charity. In answer to the requests of many priests in 1981, Mother Teresa also began the Corpus Christi Movement for Priests as a "little way of holiness" for those who desired to share in her charism and spirit.

During the years of rapid growth, the world began to turn its eyes towards Mother Teresa and the work she had started. Numerous Awards, beginning with the Indian Padmashri Award in 1962 and the Nobel Peace Prize in 1979 honored her work, while an increasingly interested media began to follow her activities. She received both prizes and attention "for the glory of God and in the name of the poor".

The whole of Mother Teresa's life and labor bore witness to the joy of loving, the greatness and dignity of every human person, the value of little things done faithfully with love and the surpassing worth of friendship with God. But there was another heroic side of this great woman that was revealed only after her death. Hidden from all eyes, hidden even from those closest to her, was her interior life marked by an experience of a deep, painful and abiding feeling of being separated from God, along with an ever-increasing longing for His Love. She called her inner experience, "the darkness." The "painful night" of her soul, which began around the time she started her work for the poor and continued to the end of her life, led Mother Teresa to an ever more profound union with God. Through the darkness, she mystically participated in the thirst of Jesus.

I personally know what it means to have the dark nights of the soul, but Mother Teresa was called to offer much greater things to the world than I. In union with Jesus' burning desire for Love, she shared in the interior desolation of the poor.

During the last years of her life, despite increasingly severe health problems, Mother Teresa continued to govern her Society and respond to the needs of the poor and the Church. By 1997, Mother Teresa's Sisters numbered nearly 4,000 members and were established in 610 foundations in 123 countries of the world.

In March 1997, she blessed her newly elected successor as Superior General of the Missionaries of Charity and then made one more trip abroad. After meeting with Pope John Paul II for the last time, she returned to Calcutta and spent her final weeks receiving visitors and instructing her Sisters. On September 5, 1997, Mother Teresa's earthly life came to an end. She was given the honor of a State Funeral by the Government of India and her body was buried in the Mother House of the Missionaries of Charity. Her tomb quickly became a place of pilgrimage and prayer for people of all faiths, rich and poor alike. Mother Teresa left a testament of unshakable faith, invincible hope and extraordinary charity. Her response to Jesus' plea, "Come be My light," made her a Missionary of Charity, a "mother to the poor," a symbol of compassion to the world and a living witness to the thirsting love of God.

Less than two years after her death, in view of Mother Teresa's widespread reputation of holiness and the favors being reported, Pope John Paul II permitted the opening of her cause of being canonized a Saint. On December 20, 2002 he approved the decrees of her heroic virtues and miracles.

Through the influence of Mother Teresa, my spiritual life made a giant leap of Faith.

THIS RITE OF PASSAGE EXPANDED MY AWARENESS TO THE DEGREE THAT ALL OF US ARE ONE BELONGING TO THE SAME DIVINE FAMILY. We should therefore be treating each other as siblings...not strangers or the enemy.

Joseph Simon Assemani

CHAPTER 11
THE ASSEMANI FAMILY

One of my Spiritual Rites of Passage
came from my own background and family
heritage. I am speaking about the Assemani

Family and my uncles, who had a profound impact on the relationship of the Vatican and the Maronites (Middle East Catholics named after St. Maron who lived in the Fifth Century.) As you may know from my other books, the name Samonie came from the Arabic name "Assemani". I have other relatives whose names are derived from the same family name, such as: Assemany, Semain, Semanie and Simony. My father happened to use "Samonie." This can easily happen when one translates from one language to another.

One of my uncles, Joseph Simon Assemani of Hasroun, Lebanon, was born in 1687. He studied at the Maronite College in Rome. He was brilliant and had an extraordinary memory. His biography stated that he was fluent in *thirty languages*.

The Vatican was aware of his unusual gifts. Soon after his ordination, he was given a post in the Vatican Library. From 1715 to 1717, he was sent to the Middle East on a manuscript expedition and the manuscripts he brought back were placed in the Vatican Library where they formed the nucleus of its subsequently famous Collection of Middle East Manuscripts. On his trip to the Middle East from 1735 to 1738, he returned with a still more valuable collection. Many extracts of the 150 manuscripts he gathered were published in his principal work, *Bibliotheca Orientalis Clemento-Vaticana* [the contents of the Middle East manuscripts in the Vatican Library].

Joseph Assemani was sent by Pope Clement XII as Papal Legate to the National Synod of Mount Lebanon in 1736. Afterwards, he was appointed Prefect of the

Vatican Library and elevated to the title of Archbishop Joseph Simon Assemani of Tyre, Lebanon. Some of his other titles were: Canon of the Basilica of St. Peter, Consultor to the Holy Office, Sigillator of the Apostolic Penitentiary (his signature was needed in cases of dispensations and indulgences) and a member of the Congregation for the Propagation of the Faith. He devoted the latter part of his life carrying out an extensive plan for editing and publishing the most valuable Syriac, Arabic, Ethiopic, Armenian, Persian, Hebrew and Greek manuscripts. Besides his various publication manuscripts in the Vatican Library, he contributed more than any other, to familiarize Europe with Syriac literature and the history of the Churches of Syria, Lebanon, Chaldea, and Egypt.

Besides his various publications on a wide range of Oriental subjects, he left about 100 works in manuscript form, some of which were destroyed in a fire in 1768, which broke out in his Vatican apartment adjacent to the Library.

Stephen Awad Assemani, nephew of Joseph Simon Assemani, completed his studies at the Maronite College in 1730. Some months later, he joined the Vatican Library as successor to his uncle. As a missionary of the Congregation for the Propagation of the Faith, he spent some time in Egypt, Syria, and Mesopotamia, where he converted the Coptic Patriarch of Alexandria and the Nestorian Patriarch of Babylon. He was consecrated an Archbishop in 1736. Pope Clement XII sent him to Florence, where he published a catalogue of the manuscripts of the Florentine Library. He later succeeded his uncle as Prefect of the Vatican Library, where he published a catalogue of its Persian and Turkish manuscripts and a large part of its Arabic manuscripts.

Elias Assemani, another member of the Assemani family, was the uncle of Joseph, who brought to Europe some of the first oriental manuscripts. Pope Clement XI sent him to the monastic libraries of Nitria, Egypt, and he returned with 40 books.

Joseph Louis Assemani, a nephew of Joseph Simon Assemani and cousin of Stephen Assemani, was an expert in Liturgy and a member of the Pontifical Academy. His nephew Simon Assemani was professor of Middle East languages at the University of Padua in Italy.

(Reprinted with permission of the Eparchy of Saint Maron, 109 Remsen Street, Brooklyn NY 11201)

Each of my uncles contributed to my spiritual Rite of Passage and a greater awareness of the religious heritage into which I was born.

When I was in the Seminary, I had a choice of choosing to be a Roman Catholic priest or a Maronite Catholic priest. I was born a Maronite, because one's Rite was passed down from the father. I would have had to study Arabic in Lebanon and study Theology also in Lebanon or in Rome. Being a direct descendant of the illustrious Assemani Family, I imagine I would have to spend my last years of study in Rome, and coming from a family of Bishops, I possibly would have had the opportunity to become one myself. Actually, I have no regrets changing from the Maronite Rite to the Latin Rite, and I am in admiration of all Bishops!

IN THIS RITE OF PASSAGE, I AM VERY HONORED AND RESPECTFUL OF MY HERITAGE, HAVING HAD SEVERAL UNCLES WHO SERVED THE CHURCH QUITE WELL WITH THEIR GOD-GIVEN TALENTS AND THEIR FAITHFUL, LIFE COMMITMENT AS BISHOPS AND ARCHBISHOPS.

Pope John XXIII

CHAPTER 12
POPE JOHN XXIII

Blessed Pope John XXIII was born
Angelo Giuseppe Roncalli at Sotto il Monte,
Italy, in the Diocese of Bergamo on

November 25, 1881. He was the fourth in a family of 14. The family worked as sharecroppers. It was a patriarchal family in the sense that the families of two brothers lived together, headed by his great uncle Zaverio, who had never married and whose wisdom guided the work and other business of the family. Zaverio was Angelo's godfather, to whom he attributed his first and most fundamental religious education. The religious atmosphere of his family and the fervent life of the parish, under the guidance of Fr. Francesco Rebuzzini, provided him with training in the Christian life.

He entered the Bergamo Seminary in 1892. Here he began the practice of making spiritual notes, which he continued in one form or another until his death, and which have been gathered together in "The

Journal of a Soul." Here he also began the deeply cherished practice of regular spiritual direction. In 1896, he was admitted to the Secular Franciscan Order by the Spiritual Director of the Bergamo Seminary, Fr Luigi Isacchi.

From 1901 to 1905 he was a student at the Pontifical Roman Seminary. On August 10, 1904, he was ordained a priest in the Church of Santa Maria located in Rome's Piazza del Popolo. In 1905 he was appointed secretary to the new Bishop of Bergamo, Giacomo Maria Radini Tedeschi. He accompanied the Bishop in his pastoral visitations and collaborated with him in his many activities: attending a Synod, managing the Diocesan Bulletin, going on pilgrimages and performing many social works. In the Seminary, he taught History, Patrology and Apologetics. He was an elegant, profound, effective and sought-after preacher.

These were the years of his deepening spiritual encounter with two Saints who were outstanding pastors: St. Charles Borromeo and St. Francis de Sales. They were years, too, of deep pastoral involvement and apprenticeship as he spent every day beside his Bishop, Radini Tedeschi. When the Bishop died in 1914, Fr. Angelo continued to teach in the Seminary and to minister in various pastoral areas.

When Italy went to war in 1915, he was drafted as a Sergeant in the Medical Corps and became a Chaplain to wounded soldiers. When the war ended, he opened a "Student House" for the spiritual needs of young people.

In 1919 he was made Spiritual Director of the Seminary, but in 1921, he was called to the service of the Holy See. Benedict XV brought him to Rome to be the Italian President of the Society for the Propagation of the Faith. In 1925, Pius XI named him Apostolic Visitator to Bulgaria, selecting him to become the Bishop of the Diocese of Areopolis. For his Episcopal motto he chose Oboedientia et Pax, (obedience and peace) which became his guiding motto for the rest of his life.

On March 19, 1925, he was actually ordained Bishop and left for Bulgaria. He was granted the title Apostolic Delegate and remained in Bulgaria until 1935, visiting Catholic Communities and establishing relationships of respect and esteem with the other Christian Communities. In the aftermath of the 1928 earthquake, he was called upon to speak to many groups that needed his sense of hope and inspiration. He endured in silence the misunderstandings and other difficulties of a Ministry on the fringes of Society and refined his sense of trust and abandonment to Jesus Crucified.

In 1935 he was named Apostolic Delegate to Turkey and Greece. The Catholic Church was present in many ways in the young Turkish Republic. His ministry among the Catholics was intense and his respectful approach and dialogue with the worlds of Orthodoxy and Islam became a feature of his tenure. When the Second World War broke out he was in Greece. He tried to get news from the prisoners of war to their families and assisted many Jews to escape by issuing "transit visas" from the Apostolic Delegation. In the month of December, 1944, Pope Pius XII appointed him *Nuncio* (a

Papal Legate of the highest rank to the government) in France.

During the last months of the war and the beginning of peace, he aided prisoners of war and helped to normalize the operation and function of the Catholic Church in France. He visited the great Shrines throughout France and participated in popular Feasts and in important religious celebrations. He was an attentive, prudent and positive observer of the new pastoral initiatives of the Bishops and clergy. His approach was always characterized by a striving for Gospel simplicity, even amid the most complex diplomatic circumstances.

The sincere piety of his interior life found expression each day in prolonged periods of prayer and meditation. In 1953, he became a Cardinal and was sent to Venice as

Patriarch. He was filled with joy at the prospect of ending his days in the direct care of souls, as he had always desired since becoming a priest. He was a wise and enterprising pastor, walking in the footsteps of St. Laurence Giustiniani, who was first Patriarch of Venice. As he advanced in years, his trust in the Lord grew in the midst of energetic, enterprising and joyful pastoral labors.

After the death of Pope Pius XII, he was elected as the next Pope on October 28, 1958, taking the name Pope John XXIII. Although he was Pope for less than five years, he was admired by the entire world as an authentic image of the Good Shepherd. Meek and gentle, enterprising and courageous, simple and active, he carried out the Christian duties of the corporal and spiritual works of mercy: *visiting the imprisoned and the sick, welcoming those of every nation and faith and bestowing on all his exquisite fatherly care.* His social perspective in the Encyclicals "Pacem in Terris" (Peace on Earth) and "Mater et Magistra" (Mother and Teacher) were deeply appreciated by a world hungry for spiritual advice and instruction from the Vatican.

To this very day, by his extraordinary example, he has helped me in seeing all God's infinite number of children as *one Son or one extension* of the Infinite Creator.

He convoked the Roman Synod, established the Commission for the Revision of the Code of Canon Law and summoned *The Second Vatican Council.*

He was present as Bishop in his Diocese of Rome through his personal visits to all his parishes, especially those in the new suburbs. The faithful saw in him a reflection of the goodness of God and called him "the good Pope". He was sustained by a profound spirit of prayer. He launched an extensive renewal of the Church, while radiating the peace of one who always trusted in the Lord. Pope John XXIII died on the evening of June 3, 1963. *MY RITE OF PASSAGE: THE EXAMPLE OF "THE GOOD POPE" LIVING AND DYING IN A SPIRIT OF PROFOUND TRUST IN JESUS AND OF LONGING FOR HIS EMBRACE.*

The world had quickly adjusted to a Pope who was not only saintly, but also very human. He was loved by everyone. Pope John XXIII was my favorite Pope. He was not afraid to open the doors to history and make changes. It is quite rare that change begins at the top. When the Pope himself says, "Let us open the windows of the Church and let some fresh air in", he was boldly facing whatever would result in a re-examination of the Dogmas and Policies of a two-thousand year Catholic Belief System.

Edgar Cayce

CHAPTER 13
EDGAR CAYCE

My encounter with the life and readings
of Edgar Cayce is somewhat unique in the
priesthood, although I am slowly discovering

that more and more priests are becoming aware of this extraordinary man. There have been several television programs in recent years portraying the life of Edgar Cayce and his psychic accomplishments. The words psychic and paranormal no longer carry the aspect of being weird, absurd, or utter nonsense. The media, in general, including books on the Best Sellers List, newspapers, the movie theaters and the internet have also given ample coverage to such topics.

Five nights each week on television, John Edward was communicating with those who had died and crossed over with messages for people in the audience. He spoke with confidence and accuracy to people he had never met before. Sylvia Browne is a popular writer – one of her books is called "Life On The Other Side" – and a TV guest who also describes in detail what life is like after death. I am not endorsing their programs, but simply making an observation that such *paranormal* activities are becoming more and more popular. The result is obvious: those who claim to be psychic demonstrate extraordinary abilities and are not challenged as openly or publicly as in the past.

Most people who believe in the paranormal usually keep it secret. However, since there are very few things kept secret about the life of the President of the United States, it was revealed that President Reagan and Nancy had an Astrologer advise them on particularly delicate issues, so as to avoid mistakes in their decisions. People laughed, but no one directly challenged the possibility that they were really helped in those situations.

A few years ago, an article in the newspaper described how many investors are seeking out assistance from a Psychic or an Astrologer, especially when the stock market started making sweeping changes regularly, sometimes losing or gaining a hundred or even two hundred points in a single day.

The evolution in awareness is moving rapidly in all circles of Society. There is an abundance of information being released every moment on this planet, but not all of the information is spiritually beneficial. To distinguish between what is real and what is imagined, calls for mature discretion and discernment. Regardless of what I know and what I have personally experienced, I am still wary of being deceived by information supposedly drawn from psychic sources. One has to tread carefully and lightly as if walking on rice paper. Rather than discarding anything that speaks of another dimension of reality, I have become very selective. What impresses me are facts that are provable and measurable. When I was teaching Mind Development Courses in the sixties and seventies, I gave the students a principle to follow. I taught them a way to change or correct undesirable thought patterns. Change is most effective when a new program, made at a deeper level of mind called the alpha dimension, is impressed on the subconscious mind. If the problem or habit were overeating, smoking, difficulty getting to sleep or whatever, they would witness success if they followed the technique as given. When students reported their surprising successes, their results were believable: instead of two packs of cigarettes per day, it was now one pack or even total abstinence from smoking. These kind of statistics are acceptable to me. They are measurable. Weight loss is measurable. The removal of headaches is measurable. These kind of results are believable.

I am impressed with the Cayce readings because they, too, are measurable. Since the readings were recorded by the stenographer Gladys Turner, it is possible to look back and examine the results of Cayce's suggestions for healing. Either what he said worked or it did not work. Fortunately, he was extremely accurate in his psychic diagnosis of people he had never seen or met.

In sharing the information in this book, I am not speaking for other clergymen. I am not the official representative of the Catholic Church. I was never appointed to that position. I speak on my own, but what I have to say comes from experience. There is no greater teacher than experience. My goal in life has always been to pursue the Truth. We all have a small portion of it. Over six billion people would like to know the Truth of who we are and why we are here. There are answers, but they all fall short of knowing or embracing Absolute Truth. Unfortunately, here on earth, we rarely or perhaps occasionally, receive a mere glimpse of Divine Truth from time to time.

For the reader who is not familiar with the life and work of Edgar Cayce, allow me to offer a brief overview of his life. Edgar Cayce was born on March 18, 1877 near Hopkinsville, Kentucky. His parents were Leslie and Carrie Cayce. Edgar was the oldest of five siblings. They were religious people belonging to a church which was a spinoff from Presbyterianism. Edgar grew up on a farm and was avidly interested in Bible stories. From the age of ten, when he received his own Bible, he read the entire Bible for every year of his life.

A few experiences in his early childhood indicate clearly that Edgar Cayce was no ordinary child and was destined for greatness. He often conversed with the spirit of his grandfather as a child (although his grandfather had died when he was four years old.) Concerning his studies in school, young Edgar discovered that by sleeping on his school book he could remember the entire contents of that book.

In a most extraordinary manner, he had a vision of a beautiful lady — perhaps the Mother of Jesus — who has been appearing around the world more and more frequently and who asked him what he would like to do.

He replied that he would like to help people. And that is precisely how he spent the rest of his life...helping people.

What took place occurred in a most surprising manner. At the turn of the century, early in the year 1900, Cayce lost the strength of his voice and for over a year could only speak in a whisper. The doctors could not help him to regain his voice. However, Al Layne, who had some basic knowledge of hypnosis, helped Cayce to enter into a self-induced trance. In the trance state, Cayce was able to speak in a normal voice, directing Al Layne how to make a verbal suggestion that would cure his condition. Layne did make such a suggestion and it was successful. Cayce was shocked when he was later told that he himself, in an unconscious state, gave the information necessary to bring about his own cure. Naturally, the question surfaced: Was it possible for Cayce to help others in the same way? After all, he had almost no knowledge of medicine; how could he prescribe anything at all? There was only one way to find out. Al Layne rented an office where they could have, what they called readings, take place. Cayce was successful from the beginning. He would leave his work as a photographer and give two readings each day. All he needed was the name of a person and his or her location. He could accurately diagnose the condition of a person anywhere on the planet and offer a suggestion or a remedy that would bring the person back to good health. He continued in this fashion for many years.

In 1923, there was a radical change in the topics presented. Rather than focusing on psychic diagnosis, Dr. Arthur Lemmers, who was also interested in Metaphysics, Religion, Philosophy and the like, added a whole new dimension to Cayce's work. In fact, it was at this time that *reincarnation* was mentioned for the first time in the readings. This caused a great deal of confusion in the awakened Cayce's mind. According to the book, "With This Gift", the story of Edgar Cayce by Anne E. Neimark, this was Cayce's first reaction to reincarnation:

"That's heresy! Souls being born again in other bodies? It's against the entire teachings of the Bible!"

"Not actually," replied Thomas Brown, one of those present. "The early Christian Fathers: St. Jerome, Plotinus, Origen...and in the late nineteenth century, the Catholic prelate Cardinal Mercier declared that the doctrine of reincarnation did not conflict with the basic teachings of the Church."

That did not help at this point. "I......I won't accept reincarnation, Edgar said. "The Bible never teaches it."

"Name me one Biblical passage that condemns it," Dr. Arthur Lammers countered.

Moments later he said, "I can't. But sensible people don't believe in souls coming back to other lives on earth."

"Yes they do, Mr. Cayce, and they have. Some of the world's greatest mental giants have accepted the doctrine; to name a few: Schopenhauer, the German philosopher, Plato, Pythagoras, Goethe, Walt Whitman and Ralph Waldo Emerson." Cayce said he needed a breather. He went outside and found a square, grassy playground...and browsed through the Bible he had probably traveled through almost fifty times. He saw the Bible in a new light.

"Except a man be born again, he cannot enter the Kingdom of God."

He also recalled that the prophet Malachi prophesied that Elijah would return before the coming of the Messiah, the Christ. Jesus told Peter, James and John that he had come already, but that people knew him not. "Then the disciples understood," as recorded in the New Testament, "that he spoke to them of John the Baptist." It appeared to be rather clear that John the Baptist was Elijah of old, reborn! He noted other quotes until his eyes grew heavy. He finally decided to trust the words from the super-intelligent readings rather than his plain, uneducated life. He stayed with Dr. Lammers for two weeks in Dayton, Ohio. By the end of the two weeks, Cayce became familiar with terms such as Karma and Karmic Law, which meant a law of spiritual cause and effect, and other metaphysical concepts.

From that point on, Edgar Cayce gave readings of either past life or health readings according to the questioner's request. Cayce had reconciled his experience of past lives with the Bible, which he knew so well.

Most of the above excerpts on Edgar Cayce's life were taken from remarks by his grandson Charles Thomas Cayce in his foreword to the book: Edgar Cayce Answers Life's 10 Most Important Questions, authored by John G. Fuller. There are many books on the complete life of Edgar Cayce. Besides "The Sleeping Prophet" by Jess Stearn and "There Is A River" by Thomas Sugrue, another excellent book, "Many Mansions", was written by a wonderful author I knew personally, Gina Cerminara. These authors each have presented the life of Cayce that differs in viewpoint from one another, completing the full picture of the man who is considered America's greatest psychic.

When Edgar Cayce died in 1945, he left behind a unique resource, complete transcripts of over 1600 readings he had given in the last decades of his life to the hundreds of people who came to him for help and advice. Subsequently, under the leadership of his son Hugh Lynn Cayce, the Association for Research and Enlightenment (A.R.E.) and the Edgar Cayce Foundation mobilized thousands of people to explore and study the transcripts which were cross-indexed in the A.R.E. Library. I believe it is the biggest Metaphysical Library in the world. I personally donated over 2,000 metaphysical books to the A.R.E. Library. These books were entrusted to my care and I passed them on to the Cayce Foundation. These books are now part of the inspiration and the teachings discovered through the Cayce readings.

Among the major themes in the readings are Alternative Health, Astrology and Reincarnation. Reincarnation, as developed in the hundreds of past-life readings given by Cayce, could be seen as the single most prominent concern of the Cayce materials. For over thirty years, Cayce went into trance and offered people information concerning their "previous lives on planet earth", while interpreting their significance for their present existence. The importance of the reincarnation theme in the Cayce readings has taken on added dimensions in this present generation with over 20 percent of the American public now professing a belief in reincarnation.

Edgar Cayce, 20th Century Psychic and Medical Clairvoyant, was another great influence in my spiritual growth and Rite of Passage. My knowledge of him came at a perfect time in my life.

For forty-three years of his adult life, Edgar Cayce demonstrated the uncanny ability to put himself into some kind of self-induced sleep state by lying down on a couch, closing his eyes and folding his hands over his stomach. This state of relaxation and meditation enabled him to place his mind in contact with all time and space. From this state he could respond to questions as diverse as "What are the secrets of the universe?"

"How can I remove a wart?"

"Have we lived another lifetime before this one?"

"What do you know about ancient Egypt?"

"What herbal roots or medication can heal this man's condition"?

His responses to these and thousands of other questions came to be called "readings". His readings contained insights so valuable that even to this day individuals have found practical help for everything from maintaining a well-balanced diet and improving human relationships to overcoming life-threatening illnesses and experiencing a closer walk with God.

Although Cayce died more than sixty years ago, the timeliness of the material in the readings is evidenced by at least a dozen biographies and more than 300 articles that discuss various aspects of this man's life and work. These books and writings contain such a huge quantity of information so valuable that even Edgar Cayce himself might have hesitated to predict their impact on the contemporary world. Sixty years ago, who could have known that terms such as *meditation, Akashic records, spiritual growth, auras, soul mates and Spirit Guides* would become household words to millions?

The majority of Edgar Cayce's readings deal with health maintenance and the treatment of illness. Yet, although best known for this material, the sleeping Cayce did not seem to be limited to concerns about the physical body. In fact, in their entirety, the readings discuss an astonishing number of 10,000 different subjects. Even this vast array of subject matter, however, can be narrowed down into a much smaller range of topics. When compiled together, the majority contain and deal with the following five categories: (1) Health-Related Information; (2) Philosophy and Reincarnation; (3) Dreams and Dream Interpretation; (4) ESP and Psychic Phenomena and (5) Spiritual Growth, Meditation, and Prayer.

My Spiritual Guidance apparently wanted me to be in contact with the Cayce readings and their metaphysical messages. I was being introduced to such considerations as: *dream interpretation, reincarnation, meditation, frequent prayer, communication with guides, the Akashic records and our superconscious minds.* I also learned about Cayce's view of a higher awareness that affirms clearly (as did Mother Teresa) that our spirits are eternal and the whole human race, without exception, are joined as the one Family of God. Whether we are aware of it or not, we are God's children, each one of us being loved unconditionally by our Infinite Creator. Learning about the Akashic Records, on which everything is recorded and can be recalled, confronts us once again about rebirth. And when an honest celebrity states facts about this life and other lifetimes, the concept of reincarnation keeps coming up as I become more deeply involved in Metaphysics.

Reincarnation is a major topic in the Cayce readings and adding my personal experiences along with them, results in a far-out spiritual Rite of Passage for me. These concerns about Reincarnation began to seriously occupy my mind in the early nineteen seventies to the extent that I became a *Life Member* of the Association of Research and Enlightenment at Virginia Beach and studying, first hand, thousands of the readings left behind as the testimony and legacy of Cayce's life.

What drew me to Cayce more than anything else, was the fact that he almost always referred to Christ. Almost every sentence refers to the Master Jesus or a quote from the Bible. *MY RITE OF PASSAGE:*

IT WAS AN EXPERIENCE OF GREAT ENLIGHTENMENT FOR ME TO KNOW THAT THERE WAS A FAMOUS PERSON WHO ALSO CENTERED HIS LIFE ON THE MASTER JESUS. He was not trying to push, so to speak, his own cause, but rather humbly attributing what good he had done for others to a Voice that spoke through him while he was in a deep sleep or trance. While awake, it was to the Lord Jesus and in Jesus' name that Cayce gave credit. Cayce was both religious and spiritual in his approach towards religion, having received the incomparable gifts that were granted to him in this lifetime.

St. Thérèse De Lisieux

CHAPTER 14
ST. THÉRÈSE DE LISIEUX;
THE LITTLE FLOWER OF JESUS

St. Thérèse de Lisieux was born in Alençon, France, the daughter of Louis Martin, a watchmaker, and Zélie-Marie

Guérin, a lacemaker. Both her parents were very religious. Louis had attempted to become a monk, but a lack of knowledge of Latin hindered him. Zélie-Marie had tried to become a nun, but was told she didn't have the vocation. Instead, she vowed that if she married, she would give all her children to the church. Louis and Zélie-Marie met in 1858 and married only three months later. They had nine children, of whom only five daughters —— Marie, Pauline, Léonie, Céline and Thérèse —— survived to adulthood since the family was subject to tuberculosis. Thérèse was their youngest child.

Her mother died of breast cancer in 1877, when Thérèse was only four years old and her father, unable to continue to work, sold his business and moved to Lisieux in the Calvados region of Normandy, where her maternal uncle Isidore Guérin, a pharmacist, lived with his wife and two daughters.

When Thérèse was nine years old, her sister Pauline, who had acted as a "second mother" to Thérèse, entered the Carmelite order of nuns. Thérèse too wanted to enter the Carmelite order, but was told she was too young. At 15, after her sister Marie also entered the same Carmelite convent, Thérèse renewed her attempts to join the order, but the priest-superior of the Convent would not allow this on account of her youth.

Her father took Thérèse on a pilgrimage to Rome. During a general audience with Pope Leo XIII, she asked him to allow her to enter the Carmelite order, but the Pope said "Well, my child, do what the superiors decide."

Shortly thereafter, the Bishop of Bayeux authorized the prioress to receive Thérèse and in April of 1888 she became a Carmelite nun. In 1889, her father suffered a stroke and was taken to a private sanatorium, where he lingered for three years. He returned to Lisieux in 1892 and died in 1894. Upon his death, her sister Céline, who had been caring for their father, entered the same Carmelite monastery as her three sisters. Her cousin, Marie Guérin, also became part of that community. Léonie, after several failed attempts, would eventually become a nun in the Order of the Visitation.

Thérèse is known for her "Little Way." In her quest for sanctity, she realized that it was not necessary to accomplish heroic acts or "great deeds" in order to attain holiness and to express her love of God. She wrote,

"Love proves itself by deeds, so how am I to show my love? Great deeds are forbidden me. The only way I can prove my love is by scattering flowers and these flowers are every little sacrifice, every glance and word and the doing of the least actions for love." This "Little Way" also appeared in her approach to spirituality:

"Sometimes, when I read spiritual treatises, in which perfection is shown with a thousand obstacles in the way and a host of illusions round about it, my poor little mind soon grows weary. I close the learned book, which leaves my head splitting and my heart parched and I take the Holy Scriptures. Then all seems luminous, a single word opens up infinite horizons to my soul; perfection seems easy. I see that it is enough to realize one's nothingness and give oneself wholly, like a child, into the arms of the good God. I leave the fine books I cannot understand to great souls and great minds. I rejoice to be little because "...only children and those who are like them, will be admitted to the heavenly banquet."

Passages like this have also left Therese open to the charge that hers is an overly sentimental and even childish spirituality. Her proponents counter that she sought to develop an approach to the spiritual life that was understandable and imitable by all who chose to do so, regardless of their level of sophistication or education.

In her last years, she rejected a spirituality that obsessed with one's faults and the imperative to "store up merits." In Therese's mature view, goodness simply meant loving God and neighbor without expecting reward or recognition. The arc of her life was away from the hypersensitivity that marred her early years towards a balanced spirituality that embraced Christ's core message.

This is evident in her approach to prayer:

"For me, prayer is a surge of the heart; it is a simple look turned toward Heaven, it is a cry of recognition and of love, embracing both trial and joy; in a word, something noble, supernatural, which enlarges my soul and unites it to God...I have not the courage to look through books for beautiful prayers...I do as a child who has not learned to read, I just tell our Lord all that I want and he understands."

Thérèse's final years were marked by a steady decline that she bore resolutely and without complaint. On the morning of Good Friday, 1896, she began bleeding at the mouth due to a pulmonary condition; her tuberculosis had taken a decided turn for the worse. Thérèse corresponded with a Carmelite mission in what was then French Indochina, and was invited to join them, but because of her sickness, she could not travel there.

In July of 1897, she was moved to the Convent infirmary where she died on September 30, 1897, at age 24. On her death-bed, she is reported to have said "I have reached the point of not being able to suffer any more, because all suffering is sweet to me."

Throughout the eighteen months before she died, Therese underwent agonizing doubts about the existence of an after-life, reporting that, despite her redoubled prayers, she feared the prospect that death would only bring about a "nothingness of being", rather than eternal life.

Thérèse de Lisieux is known today because of her spiritual autobiography, L'histoire d'une âme ("The Story of a Soul"), which she wrote upon the orders of two prioresses of her Convent. She began the work as a memoir of her childhood, under orders from her sister, Pauline, known in her Religious Order as Mother Agnes of Jesus. Mother Agnes gave the order after being prompted by their eldest sister, Sister Marie of the Sacred Heart. A second part, a letter to Sister Marie of the Sacred Heart, was written while Thérèse was on a retreat in September 1896. When the seriousness of her condition became obvious in 1896, Mother Marie de Gonzague, who succeeded Mother

Agnes as prioress, gave permission for Thérèse to finish her work. It was published posthumously and was heavily edited by her sister Pauline. (Aside from considerations of style, Mother Marie de Gonzague had ordered Pauline to alter the first two sections of the manuscript to make them appear as if they were addressed to Mother Marie as well.)

It became a devotional best-seller on account of its appealing style and on account of Therese's trust in God despite her sufferings. Since 1973, two editions of Therese's writings, including "Story of a Soul," her letters, poems, prayers and the plays she wrote for the convent recreations have been published.

In 1902, the Polish Carmelite priest Father Raphael Kalinowski (later Saint

Raphael Kalinowski) translated her autobiography "Story of a Soul" into Polish.

Pope Pius X signed the decree for the opening of her process of canonization on June 10, 1914. Pope Benedict XV, in order to hasten the process, dispensed with the usual fifty-year delay required between death and beatification. Thérèse was beatified in April, 1923 and canonized on May 17, 1925 by Pope Pius XI, only 28 years after her death. Her feast day was celebrated on October 3, until the calendar revision of 1970, when it was moved to October 1.

Thérèse of Lisieux is the patron saint of AIDS sufferers, aviators, florists, illness and missions. In 1927, Pope Pius XI named St. Therese a Patroness of the missions. In 1944, Pope Pius XII named her Co-patroness of France, along with St. Joan of Arc.

By the Apostolic Letter *Divini Amoris Scientia* ("The Science of Divine Love") of October 19, 1997, Pope John Paul II declared her one of the thirty-three Doctors of the Universal Church, one of only three women so named (the others being Teresa of Avila (Saint Teresa of Jesus) and St. Catherine of Siena). St. Thérèse was the only saint to be given recognition as a Doctor of the Church during Pope John Paul II's Pontificate.

A movement is under way now to canonize her parents, who were declared "Venerable" in 1994 by Pope John Paul II. In 2004, the Archbishop of Milan accepted the unexpected cure of a child with a lung disorder as attributable to their intercession. A date for the beatification of Louis Martin and Zelie Guerin, however, has not yet been set. Some interest has also been shown towards promoting for sainthood Thérèse's sister, Leonie, the only one of the five sisters who did not become a Carmelite nun. Leonie Martin, in religion, Sister Francoise-Thérèse, died in Caen in 1941, where her tomb in the crypt of the Visitation Convent can be visited by the public.

Together with St. Francis of Assisi, St. Thérèse of Lisieux is perhaps the most popular Catholic saint since Apostolic times. As a Doctor of the Church, she is the subject of much theological comment and study and, as an appealing young girl whose message has touched the life of millions, she remains the focus of much popular devotion.

The National Shrine of the Little Flower Catholic Church, in Royal Oak, Michigan, was built in 1925 in honor of Saint Thérèse of Lisieux. The church —— originally located in a largely Protestant area - was burned down by the Klu Klux Klan in 1936. Rebuilt out of copper and stone, a dramatic stone tower displays a 28 foot high cross bearing a figure of Jesus. On the surrounding wall is a carved portrait of Saint Thérèse of Lisieux (who was also known as the Little Flower). The Church has been declared a National Shrine, a distinction given to only a few churches in the United States.

I was very impressed when I first attended The Church of the Little Flower on Woodward Avenue, not far from my home.

MY SPIRITUAL RITE: I REALIZED THAT I DID NOT HAVE TO ACCOMPLISH GREAT THINGS TO PLEASE THE LORD. SMALL THINGS DONE WITH THE RIGHT MOTIVE OF KINDNESS, LOVE AND FORGIVENESS IN ONE'S HEART ARE BIG WITH THE LORD JESUS.

St. Therese once said: "I am a very little soul, who can offer only very little things to the Lord. I will spend my Heaven doing good on earth. After my death, I will let fall a shower of roses.

"O Jesus, my Love, my vocation, at last I have found it...my vocation is Love! Yes, I have found my place in the Church and it is You, O my God Who have given me this place; in the heart of the Church, my Mother, I shall be love."

"Everything is a grace, everything is the direct effect of our Father's love - difficulties, contradictions, humiliations, all the soul's miseries, her burdens, her needs - everything, because through them, she learns humility, realizes her weakness. Everything is a grace because everything is God's gift. Whatever be the character of life or its unexpected events - to the heart that loves, all is well."

Jesus Christ

CHAPTER 15
MY PERSONAL ENCOUNTERS
WITH THE LORD JESUS

Naturally, each time I received a personal visit by my Master Jesus, it was a spiritual Rite of Passage for me. It was as if

I had made my most exciting retreat and I was on cloud nine!

So many people had expressed to me their great desire to have a single encounter with the Lord Jesus. Those who make such a statement should be overjoyed and even overwhelmed knowing that Jesus, a Universal Spirit, is the Master Teacher to everyone on the planet. Every human being is guided by the Lord Jesus and the Holy Spirit.

Unfortunately, most people fail to recognize His Presence; He responds to every call in His Name. He is also invited to be at your presence and be your Divine Helper through prayer and meditation. How I wish everyone were aware of His Divine Presence everywhere and at all times. Just knowing that the Lord Jesus has even made one single visit to you personally — and He has many times! — should increase everyone's *faith* a hundred percent!

Remembering that we are all members of God's Family and that Jesus is our Elder Brother Who is constantly forever watching over us, the whole world would change overnight, believing in God, the Christ and the Holy Spirit. It would shut down the imagined separation between this world and the Eternal Kingdom of God. This world would be Heavenly. When people of every religion would know in their minds and in their hearts that God, Allah, Yahweh are the one and same God and His Messengers are all working for the same cause, it would add greatly to world peace. Jesus, Mohammad, Buddha, Ramakrishna and others have been sent here by the very same God and Creator of every human being. We are siblings, not enemies. The result would be *ONE GIGANTIC, UNIVERSAL AND SPIRITUAL RITE OF PASSAGE THE WORLD HAD NEVER BEFORE WITNESSED.*

We would no longer have a deep sense of separation from God nor from each other. There would be no talk of a great and decisive battle at Armageddon, nor would anyone be considered separate and, therefore, left behind. We would all be as the One Creation/Son of God...which we are and shall always be! In God's World, that can never change. Heaven is not a place nor a condition; it is an awareness of Reality.

My first vision of Jesus was seeing Him as a very young Child being held up with one hand by St. Joseph in a vision which lasted for over an hour. The wonderful vision was seen by myself and three of my siblings over Mt. Elliott Cemetery in Detroit, Michigan. We lived across the street from the Cemetery, overlooking it from the window of the second floor. The second-story apartment was owned by our parents as well as the grocery store just below us. At the time, Rose was 15, Billie 12, Tony 10 and I was the youngest, just 7 years old. We had no school that day because it was the Feast of the Ascension of Jesus into Heaven. It was a Holy Day! I only saw the Child Jesus from a distance. We did not speak.

The second visit with the Lord Jesus took place in St. Bernadette Church in Southwest Dearborn in the late sixties. This time I saw Jesus in His true state: *a Being of Divine Light.* During this visit, His Magnificent Presence lit up the whole Church and I had a feeling of being in a huge Cathedral instead of the tiny matchbox shaped chapel called St. Bernadette's Church.

I fell to my knees and wept. Although my soul and spirit were extremely excited at the thought of being visited by Someone from Heaven, I felt terribly unworthy to be in His Presence. How could I remain standing in the presence of such greatness? Surprisingly, when I opened my eyes and looked up again, He gently motioned for me to stand. Slowly I arose to my feet, but the tears, I couldn't stop. He made no judgement upon me, but I knew that He was aware of everything good or bad I had done in my entire lifetime. *I WAS LOVED UNCONDITIONALLY. IN HUMAN TERMS, I NEVER KNEW EXACTLY WHAT THAT MEANT. THIS WAS ONE OF MY GREATER SPIRITUAL RITES OF PASSAGE, GIFTED BY THE MASTER*

HIMSELF. This memorable date was November 17, 1970.

The visits continued. That same night I had the first of the forty consecutive nights in which I had mystical and spiritual experiences. This happened more than 35 years ago. Since then, many people have written about their experiences of going through what may be called a tunnel and going to the other side. They speak of a beautiful and heavenly place where they wanted to stay, but were told that they had to come back to earth. Their life work was not yet completed.

My situation was quite different. I did go through a tunnel when a huge eye appeared in my room at 4:00 a.m. The eye, which seemed to be embroidered in gold, kept increasing in size as it was coming toward me. The pupil of the eye, totally black, engulfed me and I suddenly left my physical body and thought for sure that I had died. Instead, I found myself going through the tunnel leaving me alone out in deep space. I was well beyond the moon and the earth. I didn't know what to do! Before I was able to become totally confused and disoriented, the Lord Jesus immediately appeared at my side and took me by the hand. He calmly said, "Do not be afraid!" And all fear left me immediately! We went on a COSMIC JOURNEY through the Universe, passing many star systems, galaxies and nebulas. What I had witnessed was the stunning and incredible Cosmos, never before seen by a human, as far I know. *IT IS DIFFICULT EVEN TO DESCRIBE THIS SPIRITUAL RITE OF PASSAGE SINCE WE WERE BOTH IN A SPIRITUAL BODY — NOT RESTRICTED BY A PHYSICAL ONE — AND IT*

WAS A JOURNEY OF AN INCREDIBLE DISTANCE.

Then the Lord Jesus took me back to St. Bernadette Church Rectory and slowly and gently put me back into my physical body (which, by the way, was sound asleep and snoring!)

A more recent visit by my Lord and Master Jesus happened about ten days after my stroke, when I was in the process of dying and going to the other side. Again, remembering what happened to the small church at St. Bernadette when the Presence of Christ made it appear to be a huge Cathedral. It happened once again! what seemed to be a small, dark hospital room with a low ceiling turned into a large, bright and beautiful hall with a very high doorway rounded at the top. *Apparently, I did die* and was in a hospital in the afterlife. It was heavenly place; however, Jesus walked in, came up to me and said, "You have to go back. It is not your time yet, my son." *RITE OF PASSAGE: I WAS CALLED BACK FROM THE DEAD.*

My desire was to die and go Home to God's Eternal Kingdom. My body was already a corpse, paralyzed, unable to move, talk or eat anything. All IVs had to be removed from my body. At that time, I even prayed to die! I had no more movement than a corpse and I wanted to go Home.

"Please Lord, can't you take me Home now?"

He said very clearly, "My son, I did not come to take you Home! You will recover and you will be called Home after you do and experience certain things still planned for you." I was unhappy to suddenly find myself back on earth in that same dark, tiny hospital bed.

I didn't imagine recovery was even possible. But I did. Since the Lord Jesus healed me, I began to recover that very next morning. The process of recovery has been slow. However, I have managed to keep my mind active, even though I became a shut-in. I continued to read, do puzzles, paint and play the piano. During my illness and recovery, I have even written and published my fourth book, "The Holy Spirit: Our Divine Companion Guiding Us On Our Way Home." What you are now reading is my fifth book.

While many very religious and prayerful folks are seriously waiting for the Second Coming of Jesus Christ, I wonder if it is necessary to pray for His return since He has actually never left us. I have read about the lives of saintly men and women who have revealed in their writings that they were guided by Christ Himself. These were not just ordinary people. They themselves have testified to the Presence of Christ and most of them have been canonized officially as Saints by the Church in the last two thousand years.

Obviously, Jesus has been very active here on earth during the last two thousand years. My own private testimony, based on actual experience, tells me that the Lord Jesus and the Holy Spirit have always been here helping anyone who calls for spiritual help...regardless of their color, race, culture or belief system.

Also, I have never forgotten Jesus' powerful words which are the last lines of St. Matthew's Gospel: *"And know that I am with you always,* until the end of the world." The universal image of Jesus, sent by God as Master Teacher and Miracle-worker, lived among us doing good for so many people. Although His followers identified Him as the Christ, He was betrayed by one of His own and was handed over to His enemies to be tortured and crucified. Having risen from the dead, He now sits at the right hand of the Father. This is the basis of Christian teaching.

Certain denominations of Christians, however, are obsessed with a strong hope and desire that He will return soon into our world to do battle with evil forces at Armageddon to decide whether the world will be dominated by the Lord Jesus Christ or by the Anti-Christ. I do not believe we are going to witness such a battle in our lifetime.

The final and complete destruction of evil forces is just as mysterious as predicting the end of the world. (And Jesus said that only the Father knows when the world will end.) Until then, the Lord Jesus and the Holy Spirit make themselves known to us when we are filled with a spiritual hunger and desire for Their Presence; in other words, when we are ready for a serious spiritual Rite of Passage. That is His Second Coming: to each of us individually.

During the period of my recovery, the Lord Jesus and the Holy Spirit have appeared and spoke to me on several occasions. At other times, I did not see them, but heard their voices very clearly. Contrary to what Tradition or History tells us, they are very active in the world. They are the Master Teacher and Guide to every human being. It is also obvious that They are both Divinely happy and, at times, even display a sense of humor.

I hesitate to tell you the following since we tend to think of a Divine Person as totally serious. What I am about to say was my actual experience:

The Lord Jesus and the Holy Spirit played a joke on me for my birthday. I was 76 years old on April 27, 2006. It was a rather uneventful day and I went to sleep at my usual hour. However, in the middle of the night, around 4:00 a.m., I was awakened by someone's laughter. I did not see anyone!

I said, "Is this laughter coming from the two Divine Guests Who happened to visit me before?" (Meaning Jesus and the Holy Spirit)

Jesus then became clearly visible and replied, "yes, and we are laughing because we played a joke on you for your birthday!"

"A joke! What kind of a joke?" Frankly, I was surprised that they even thought about my birthday.

"We arranged something for you on your birthday. You hardly play the lottery anymore. Too bad! However, when you read today's newspaper you will see that your birthday came out in the first lottery and your age came out in the evening...the very same day...on your birthday!"

"That could just happen by chance!" I replied.

"Not likely!" He said. "The odds of this happening on your birthday the very same day is staggering."

"So, what are the odds? A thousand to one?", I asked innocently, about playing the odds.

"Much higher!" He said as He laughed.

"A million to one odds?" I asked.

"No! *Nine million to one odds* for that to happen to you on your 76th birthday. We set it up! Working with the Father/Creator, nothing is impossible.

"Why didn't you tell me the day before?" I questioned.

"We know you only too well, my son. You would have gone to the nearest Lottery store and invested enough to make a million dollars. This was not done to help you make a lot of money. It was a joke to let you know we are always present."

That was true! I would have spent a lot of money on the lottery if I knew in advance what the results would be. (Well, my dear reader, "Wouldn't you?") *THE MASTER JESUS AND THE HOLY SPIRIT QUICKLY REMINDED ME ONCE AGAIN THAT THEIR PURPOSE WAS TO EDUCATE ME SPIRITUALLY AND TO GUIDE ME TO A GREATER AWARENESS OF TRUTH AND REALITY THROUGH MY SPIRITUAL RITES OF PASSAGE.* Making money was not an issue!

He said He could make me a millionaire tomorrow or any day, if that was His purpose!

If you could just once see Jesus smiling and speaking to you personally, you would never be frightened in His Presence. He has a way of gently capturing your heart through unconditional Love and the Joy and the Peace that continually surround His Presence. And He is always present, whether or not you see Him or hear Him!

Our Lady of Guadalupe

CHAPTER 16
OUR LADY OF GUADALUPE

In the Americas or the New World in 1521, the capital city of the Aztec Empire fell under the Spanish forces. Ten years later, nine million of the inhabitants of the land, who professed for centuries a polytheistic and human-sacrificing religion, were converted to Christianity. What happened in those times that produced such an unprecedented and historically incredible conversion?

At dawn on December 9, 1531, on Tepeyác Hill near Mexico City, Our Blessed Lady (The Mother of Jesus) appeared to Juan Diego, an Aztec Indian. While on his way to attend Mass, he heard sounds of chirping birds and beautiful music and wondered where it was coming from and its meaning. Then he heard a voice calling him and She revealed Herself as "the Ever Virgin Mother of the True God" and made known Her desire that a Shrine be built there to bear witness to Her love, Her compassion and Her protection. She sent him to Bishop Juan de

Zumárraga in Mexico City to request Her great desire. The Bishop insisted on some proof that She was the Mother of Jesus. She appeared to Juan Diego again and directed him to pick the fresh roses near him and to place them in his winter coat or tilma. It is a fact that roses do not grow in the winter in Tepeyác.

After waiting for a long time to see the Bishop, he finally entered the Bishop's office and opened his tilma. The fresh roses fell to the floor and the Bishop and his Staff immediately fell to their knees. Juan Diego was surprised! What he did not know was that not only were the fresh roses proof of Who She was, but Our Lady of Guadalupe had an image of Herself being painted miraculously on his tilma directly in front of them. The Bishop was convinced and had Her Shrine built.

His coat or tilma, a poor quality cactus-cloth, which should have deteriorated in 20 years, showed no sign of decay after 475 years and still defies all scientific explanations of its origin. There is no other paint on earth like the substance of the paint used in the image.

The miraculous painting of Our Lady of Guadalupe even reflects in her eye the image of Juan Diego who was her messenger in 1531!

Her message of love and compassion and Her universal promise of help and protection to all humankind, as well as the story of the apparitions, are described in the "Nican Mopohua", a 16th century document written in the native Nahuatl language.

An incredible list of miracles, cures and interventions are attributed to Her. Every year an estimated 10 million people visit Her Basilica, making her Mexico City home the most popular Marian Shrine in the world and the most visited Catholic Church in the world, next to the Vatican.

Altogether, 25 popes have officially honored Our Lady of Guadalupe. His Holiness John Paul II visited her Sanctuary four times: on his first apostolic trip outside Rome as Pope in 1979, again in 1990, 1999 and in 2002, the same year in which Juan Diego was canonized St. Juan Diego by the Pope.

The Feast of Our Lady of Guadalupe is celebrated on December 12th. In 1999, Pope John Paul II, in his homily from the Solemn Mass at the Basilica of Our Lady of Guadalupe during his third visit to the sanctuary, declared the date of December 12th as a Liturgical Holy Day for the whole continent.

During the same visit Pope John Paul II entrusted the cause of life to Her loving protection and placed under Her motherly care the innocent lives of children, especially those who are in danger of not being born.

MY RITE OF PASSAGE AT THE BASILICA DEDICATED TO OUR LADY OF GUADALUPE IN MEXICO WAS ANOTHER GIANT STEP IN AWARENESS AND UNDERSTANDING OF REALITY. While I was in line to see the miraculous picture up close, Our Lady of Guadalupe stepped out of the picture and stood right in front of me. She altered any other objectives I had as a priest when She said, *"MI HIJITO, CUIDA MI GENTE." ("MY*

DEAR SON, TAKE CARE OF MY PEOPLE.") I was not ordained a priest yet, but I was told what my mission as a priest would be...working with the Hispanic Community, which I did until my retirement in 1995. IT WAS A RITE OF PASSAGE I LOVED AND I WOULD NEVER FORGET! I studied Spanish diligently, I spoke Spanish fluently and I chose to stay in the inner city of Detroit, where Hispanic Communities existed.

Each year, on December 12, I celebrated Mass in honor of Our Lady of Guadalupe and each year I gave a talk about her. I became very emotional when I mentioned her name and the whole story of how she appeared to St. Juan Diego and influenced Bishop Zumárraga to build a Cathedral her name. Of course, she had to work a few miracles to make it happen. Today, Our Lady of Guadalupe is considered the Patroness of all the Americas. I have come to refer to Her as my "mamacita" (My dear mother) whenever I pray to Her.

I took my mission from my mamacita very seriously and without explaining to the Assignment Board, turned down an offer to be Pastor of one of the largest and wealthiest parishes in the Archdiocese of Detroit at that time.

I agreed to go to Holy Trinity in the inner city instead. It was in the center of the Mexican and other Hispanic Communities...*Our Lady of Guadalupe's people*!

I was amazed a few years ago when something unusual happened to the rose bush Ben Duckworth and his wife Barbara (of happy memory) gave to me as a gift. It was called *Our Lady of Guadalupe Rose.* That year, on December 12, the Feast Day of Our Lady of Guadalupe, all flowers outdoors had naturally died...except one flower, the Guadalupe rose. It was in full bloom on her Feast Day. It was not a miraculous event, but I took it as a message of love from my mamacita.

Jiddu Krishnamurti

CHAPTER 17
KRISHNAMURTI

Jiddu Krishnamurti (born May 12, 1895, Madanapalle, Andhra Pradesh, India, and died on February 18, 1986, at Ojai,

California). He was born of middle-class Brahmin parents and was recognized at age fourteen by the Theosophists, Annie Besant and C.W. Leadbeater, as the next *World Teacher*. Mrs. Besant adopted the boy and took him to England, where he was educated and prepared for his coming role.

He was made head of her newly formed worldwide religious organization, the Order of the Star in the East in 1911, but in 1929 after many years of questioning himself, he dissolved the Order, repudiated its claims and returned all the assets given to him for its purpose. Out of his own spiritual "process", experienced from 1922 onwards, he declared and this became a *RITE OF PASSAGE FOR ME*: "*TRUTH IS A PATHLESS LAND AND YOU CANNOT APPROACH IT BY ANY PATH WHATSOEVER, BY ANY RELIGION OR BY ANY SECT. TRUTH, BEING LIMITLESS,*

UNCONDITIONED, UNAPPROACHABLE BY ANY PATH WHATSOEVER, CANNOT BE ORGANIZED." He continued, "Nor should any organization be formed to lead or to coerce people along any particular path. My only concern is to set humanity absolutely, unconditionally free. One cannot come to it through any organization, through any creed, through any dogma, priest or ritual, not through any philosophic knowledge or psychological technique. One has to find it through the understanding of the contents of one's own mind, through observation and not through intellectual analysis."

Krishnamurti claimed allegiance to no caste, nationality or religion and was bound by no tradition. He traveled the world and spoke spontaneously to large audiences until the end of his life at age ninety. He said we must free ourselves of all fear and conditioning through self-knowledge and this will bring about order and psychological change. This conflict-ridden and violent world cannot be transformed into a life of goodness, love and compassion by any political, social or economic strategies, but only through the change in individuals brought about through their own observation.

In observing this content, we discover within ourselves the division of the *observer* and what is *observed*. He points out that this division, which prevents direct perception, is the root of human conflict.

Heads of various religious organizations held discussions with him, only to hear him repeat his central theme that authority in whatever form — religious, psychological or political —- is a hindrance to seeing the truth. Man has to be his own guru to bring about psychological transformation. In 1984, he spoke to nuclear scientists at the National Laboratory Research Center at Los Alamos, New Mexico, U.S.A. David Bohm Ph.D., the quantum physicist and friend of Einstein, recognized that Krishnamurti`s teachings parallel with his own revolutionary theories of physics. This led to many years of dialogue between the two men, which helped form a bridge between so-called mysticism and science. Other scientists found his discussions of *time, thought and death* to be thought-provoking.

Krishnamurti said, "Surely a school is a place where one learns about the *totality, the wholeness of life.* Academic excellence is absolutely necessary, but a school includes much more than that. It is a place where both the *teacher and the student* explore not only the outer world, the world of knowledge, but also their own thinking, their behavior." Freedom from conditioning and its misery begins with this awareness (Rite of Passage). He established foundations in India, Europe and the United States.

In 1969 the Krishnamurti Foundation of America (KFA) was created in the Ojai Valley by Krishnamurti and several Trustees. KFA`s Mission was, and still is, to protect and disseminate Krishnamurti`s teachings during and after his lifetime. KFA is also responsible for the Oak Grove School, founded by Krishnamurti and the Foundation in 1975. The school was started with the serious intention to create a unique learning environment that would meet the needs of children facing a world in conflict. The school started with three students in 1975 and presently has an enrollment of 175 learners from pre-kindergarten to 12th grade.

The Archives Building contains a comprehensive record of Krishnamurti`s teachings, including all of his books and an extensive selection of talks and interviews on audio and video tapes. The building also offers a peaceful and harmonious place to work, while providing researchers and scholars access to original manuscripts, thousands of audio and video recordings, 7000 photographs, 5000 letters, books in 22 languages, films, newspaper articles and other materials for research.

Some of his popular books are: "Commentaries On Living", "The Awakening Of Intelligence", "The First And Last Freedom", "Think On These Things", and "The Ending Of Time".

Pope John Paul II

CHAPTER 18
POPE JOHN PAUL II

To Catholics, he was the Universal Shepherd. To world leaders, he was able to bring moral support or stinging criticism.

Non-Christians around the globe have welcomed him as a holy guest. Poor nations consider him their advocate in the halls of power. And for nearly everyone, he's been a voice of conscience on issues like war, abortion and the death penalty.

The world knows Pope John Paul II in different dimensions: manager, missionary, statesman and prophet. His message was not always easy and his words were not always welcome. But it's hard to imagine a more influential figure on the global scene over the last twenty-five years.

If his pontificate seems a perfect match for our age, perhaps it's because he experienced its joys and trials firsthand – as no previous Pontiff has.

The path to the Papacy was not a simple one for Karol Wojtyla. As a youth in southern Poland, he studied at the University, acted in a clandestine theater, wrote poetry and read philosophy, played goalie on his soccer team, split stone at a quarry and worked in a chemical factory. Only then did his vocation to the priesthood come into focus.

"I had positive experiences in many settings and from many people and God's voice reached me through them," the Pope said in his 1996 book, "Gift and Mystery".

The Pope's early life was marked by personal hardships and shadowed by national tragedies. Born on May 18, 1920, in the small town of Wadowice south of Krakow, the future Pope lost his mother, Emilia, when he was nine years of age. Her death was an event that stayed with him and acquaintances say it prompted his lifelong spiritual devotion to the Virgin Mary. One of his first youthful poems, "Over This, Your White Grave," was dedicated to his mother's memory.

Three years later, his only brother, Edmund, a physician, died of scarlet fever. At the age of twenty, he lost his father, a military officer who had raised his son with love and firmness. Young Karol would sometimes wake in the middle of the night and find his father praying on his knees. At his death, friends say Karol knelt for twelve hours in prayer at his father's bedside.

The Pope's former schoolmates describe him as friendly, but pensive: an athletic youth who excelled in academics and spent a lot of time in church. They noticed the intense way he prayed – a habit of deep meditation that remained with him for life. One companion good-naturedly called him an "apprentice saint."

"Even as a boy he was exceptional," said Rafat Tatka, a neighbor who knew the young boy as Lolek, a nickname that translates as Chuck. Growing up, the Pope was especially protective of his Jewish friends.

As a teenager, he was already showing an appetite for philosophy and an amazing talent for languages. In 1938, he began working toward a Degree in Philosophy at the University of Krakow and was an active member of speech and drama clubs.

All that was interrupted by the Nazi invasion of Poland on September 1, 1939, which devastated the country and left an indelible impression on nineteen-year-old Karol Wojtyla. A priest later described how Wojtyla arrived at the Cathedral when the first German bombs started to fall and attended Mass amid the howl of sirens and the blasts of explosions.

With official schools closed during the German occupation, he helped set up an underground university and the clandestine "Rhapsodic Theater," which met in members' apartments. To make ends meet, he also took a job at the local Solvay quarry and chemical factory. More than fifty years later, he described how a fellow laborer was killed by flying rock, a "sense of injustice" emanating from his lifeless body. The Pope himself was nearly killed when he was hit by a truck near the plant and remained unconscious for several hours. Karol Wojtyla had women friends, especially in the theater circles. Some thought that's why his vocation came relatively late in life.

But as he once explained it, a girlfriend "wasn't the problem". What delayed his entry to the priesthood was his great passion for Literature, Philosophy and Drama – but the war helped change that, too.

He started noticing that some of his friends had disappeared, killed in war or seized in the night by Nazi troops. It haunted him.

On the fiftieth anniversary of his ordination, he wrote, "Any day I could have been picked up on the street, at the factory or at the stone quarry and sent to a concentration camp. Sometimes I asked myself: *so many people at my age were losing their lives, why not me?"*

He gradually came to feel that he was spared for a higher reason, part of a Divine Plan to bring something good out of wartime Poland.

"I know it wasn't just chance," he said. If his Polish friends and neighbors were being sacrificed on the "altar of history," he would dedicate his life to God and the Church. The decision was a blow to his student companions, but he hoped they would understand in time.

He entered Krakow's clandestine Theological Seminary in 1942, a risky step under the Gestapo's watchful eyes. Always drawn to the mystical and contemplative, at one point he considered joining the local

Carmelite Order instead of being a parish priest. But his cardinal told him: "Finish what you've begun" and the Carmelite Director is said to have turned him away with the words: "You are destined for greater things!"

Four years later he was ordained, just as Poland was passing from the nightmare of Nazi occupation to the ideological vise-grip of a new Communist regime. Father Wojtyla was sent to study at Rome's Angelicum University, where he did course work in Ethics and wrote a thesis on St. John of the Cross, a sixteenth-century mystic.

Back in Poland in 1948, the young priest got his first assignment to the rural village of Niegowic, twenty miles outside of Krakow. In what would become typical fashion, he walked there through the fields during harvest time – and kissed the ground when he arrived. A year later, he became Pastor of St. Florian Parish in Krakow, devoting much of his ministry to young people. He taught them, played soccer, took them on hikes and invited them to his house for discussions.

Father Wojtyla turned to Academics again, earning a second Doctorate in Moral Theology. In 1953, he began commuting to Lublin University to teach. By the time he reached his mid-thirties, he had published dozens of articles and several books on Ethics. But he also made time to write poems and plays.

Father Wojtyla loved being outdoors and he enjoyed taking groups of students hiking, skiing, camping and canoeing in the hills of southern Poland. He took off his collar and told the youth to call him "uncle", because it was illegal for priests to sponsor such outings under Communism.

He was on a kayaking trip in 1958 when he was named an Auxiliary Bishop of Krakow. At the time, he was 38 years old and the youngest Bishop in Polish History. He shunned the trappings of the new position, however, and left his humble apartment for the more comfortable Bishops' residence, only after friends moved his belongings there one day when he was out of town.

In 1964, he was named Archbishop of Krakow, and three years later became a Cardinal, one of the youngest in the Church. He spent much of his first two years as Cardinal commuting to Rome for the final session of the Second Vatican Council, where he helped draft the outstanding and landmark document "Gaudium et Spes" (The Church in the Modern World).

Cardinal Wojtyla was very much in line with the Vatican Council's push to tear down the walls between the church and the world and make Faith an everyday experience. But that did not mean turning his back on the Church's traditional teachings – far from it.

In the mid 1960's, he helped advise Pope Paul VI on sexual morality issues and he eventually helped prepare the controversial encyclical "Humanae Vitae" (On Human Life), which upheld the Church's teaching against birth control.

Respected in the Vatican's inner circle, but virtually unknown to the rest of the world, Cardinal Karol Wojtyla was elected Pope on October 16, 1978. He was the Church's first non-Italian Pontiff in 455 years and most people didn't recognize his name when it was announced in St. Peter's Square — they thought he was African. But his fluency in Italian won the crowd over that night, and got his Papacy off to a running start. Within months, he had taken trips around the globe, held airborne press conferences, issued an encyclical on *"Redemption"*, met with world leaders and opened a new chapter in ecumenical dialogue with the Orthodox Church.

This hurricane pace was slowed by a would-be assassin's bullets on May 13, 1981. Mehmet Ali Agca, a Turkish terrorist, shot the Pope as he was riding in his jeep in St. Peter's Square. The Pontiff was rushed to a Rome hospital and underwent hours of surgery. The Pope later deposited the bullet fragments in the crown of a statue of Our

Lady of Fatima, whose feast day is May 13, and said he owed his life to Mary. Two and a half years after the shooting, he visited Agca in his Italian prison cell in a remarkable act of forgiveness and reconciliation.

The Pope was soon back in full swing, in a Papacy that has rewritten the record books. He's logged more than 700,000 miles in trips to nearly 130 countries, including such remote spots as Azerbaijan, with a Catholic population of 120.

Many credit his political activity and his morale-boosting trips to Poland as a major role in helping to bring down European Communism in 1989. In a historic meeting with Soviet Premier Mikhail Gorbachev, the Pope nurtured the Glasnost Reform policy that would eventually lead to the break-up of the Soviet empire.

In other parts of the world, he prodded dictators and pleaded for human rights. At the same time, he lectured Liberation Theologians and warned Bishops and priests against confusing the Gospel with political ideology. His social encyclicals challenged the architects of the globalized free-market economy to narrow the gap between the rich and the poor in the world.

Despite some people's misgivings about Church Teachings like birth control and the all-male priesthood, he received warm welcomes in his seven trips to the United States, where he was cheered by half a million young people in Denver in 1993.

Pope John Paul II has carried the pro-life banner proudly. Throughout the last decade he has urged bishops and lay Catholics to fight abortion and euthanasia, saying the "slaughter of the innocents" must be stopped. He's also argued that moral justification for the death penalty is practically nonexistent in the modern age, and his interventions have sometimes helped save the lives of death-row inmates. Not everyone agrees with the Pope's public pronouncements, but popularity has never been his goal.

"The Pope becomes a persona non grata (a person not appreciated or liked) when he tries to convince the world of human sin," he said with a dose of realism in 1994.

Yet, more than any previous Church leader, he has earned near-universal respect for highlighting moral and ethical values and for speaking out on behalf of the millions of people who have little or no voice in global affairs.

Battling fatigue and illness in later years, the Pope kept up a remarkable string of initiatives inside the Church as well. He used the Holy Year in 2000 to celebrate every aspect of the faith, apologize for Christians' historic misdeeds and map out a pastoral strategy for the new millennium.

He broke down interfaith barriers when he visited a Jewish Synagogue, a Muslim Mosque and made pilgrimages to Orthodox countries where no pope had ever set foot. He convened unprecedented "prayer summits" in the Italian hill town of Assisi and orchestrated interreligious condemnations of terrorism.

Increasingly, he has emphasized to his own flock that prayer is powerful and that personal holiness can change the world.

In a typical blend of the traditional and the new, he recently reformed the praying of the rosary, formulating five new "Mysteries of Light". And he's canonized more than 470 new Saints, including lay people from various walks of life to illustrate his message that true Faith is faith in action.

In ways big and small, he has left a lasting image on his Church: in written documents and dramatic gestures, in doctrinal firmness and heartfelt prayer, and by naming nearly all the Cardinals who will one day choose his successor. Many young Catholics, who have never known another Pope, call themselves part of the "John Paul II generation."

Despite his frailty, the Pope intended to keep bringing the light of the Gospel to the great issues of the twenty-first century. It's a ministry he had carried out with the halting steps of an old man and the determination of an Apostle. In final battle with ill health, he died with honor and dignity.

THERE WERE MANY SPIRITUAL RITES OF PASSAGE I LEARNED FROM POPE JOHN PAUL II. ONE OF THEM WAS NOT TO BE AFRAID! I HAVE WRITTEN AT THIS TIME, FOUR PUBLISHED BOOKS. SOME OF THE MATERIAL MAY BE CONSIDERED CONTROVERSIAL, BUT I TRUST IN THE LORD TO TELL THE TRUTH AS I UNDERSTAND IT FROM MY STUDIES AND FROM MY PERSONAL EXPERIENCE. I have never written anything I have not believed in or experienced!

Rabindranath Tagore

CHAPTER 19
TAGORE

Rabindranath Tagore was considered the greatest writer in modern Indian literature. He was a Bengali poet, novelist, educator and an early advocate of Independence for India. Tagore won the Nobel Prize for Literature in 1913. Two years later, he was elevated to the status of Knighthood, but he surrendered it in 1919 as a protest against the Massacre of Amritsar, where British troops killed some 400 Indian demonstrators. Tagore's influence over Gandhi and the founders of modern India was enormous, but his reputation in the West as a mystic has perhaps mislead his Western readers to ignore his role as a reformer and critic of colonialism.

"When one knows thee, then alien there is none, then no door is shut. Oh, grant me my prayer that I may never lose touch of the one in the play of the many." (from Gitanjali)

Rabindranath Tagore was born in 1861. He came from a wealthy and prominent family in Calcutta. His father was Maharishi Debendranath Tagore, a religious reformer and scholar. His mother, Sarada Devi, died when Tagore was very young - he realized that she would never come back when her body was carried through a gate to a place where it was burned. Tagore's grandfather had established a huge financial empire for himself. He supported a number of public projects, such as Calcutta Medical College.

The Tagores tried to combine traditional Indian culture with Western ideas; all their children contributed significantly to Bengali literature and culture. However, in his "My Reminiscences", Tagore mentions that it was not until the age of ten that he started to use socks and shoes. Tagore, the youngest, started to compose poems at the age of eight. Tagore's first book, a collection of poems, appeared when he was 17. It was published by Tagore's friend who wanted to surprise him.

Tagore received his early education first from tutors and then at a variety of schools. Among them were the Bengal Academy, where he studied History and Culture. At University College, London, he studied Law but left after a year - he did not like the weather. It was known that he once gave a beggar a gold coin - it was more than the beggar had expected and he returned it. In England, Tagore started to compose the poem 'Bhagna Hridaj' (a broken heart).

In 1883, Tagore married Mrinalini Devi Raichaudhuri, with whom he had two sons and three daughters. In 1890, Tagore moved to East Bengal (now Bangladesh), where he collected local legends and folklore. Between 1893 and 1900, he wrote seven volumes of poetry, including "SONAR TARI" (The Golden Boat), 1894 and "KHANIKA" in 1900. This was a highly productive period in Tagore's life and earned him the rather misleading epitaph "The Bengali Shelley." More important was that Tagore wrote in the common language of the people. This also was something that was hard to accept among his critics and scholars.

Tagore was the first Indian to bring an element of psychological realism to his novels. Among his early major prose works are "NASHTANIR", (The Broken Nest) in 1901, "CHOCHER BALI" (Eyesore) in 1903 and published first serially. Between 1891 and 1895, he published forty-four short stories in Bengali periodicals, most of them in the monthly journal Sadhana.

Tagore's short stories deeply influenced Indian Literature. "Punishment", a much anthologized work, was set in a rural village. It describes the oppression of women through the tragedy of the low-caste Rui family.

In 1901, Tagore founded a school outside Calcutta, named Visva-Bharati, which was dedicated to emerging Western and Indian philosophy and education. It become a university in 1921.

Tagore's reputation as a writer was established in the United States and in England. Tagore's poems were also praised by Ezra Pound and drew the attention of the Nobel Prize committee. "There is in him the stillness of nature. The poems do not seem to have been produced by storm or by ignition, but seem to show the normal habit of his mind. He is at one with nature, and finds no contradictions. This is in sharp contrast with the Western mode, where man must be shown attempting to master nature if we are to have "great drama". (Ezra Pound in Fortnightly Review, March 1, 1913) However, Tagore also experimented with poetic forms and these works have lost much in translations into other languages.

Much of Tagore's ideology came from the teaching of the Upanishads and from his own beliefs that God can be found through personal purity and service to others. He stressed the need for new world order based on transnational values and ideas, the "unity consciousness." "The soil, in return for her service, keeps the tree tied to her; the sky asks nothing and leaves it free." Politically active in India, Tagore was a supporter of Gandhi, but warned of the dangers of nationalistic thought. Unable to gain ideological support to his views, he retired into relative solitude. Between the years 1916 and 1934 he traveled widely. From his journey to Japan in 1916, he produced articles and books. In 1927, he toured in Southeast Asia. He produced a book, "JATRI", in 1929. His Majesty, Riza Shah Pahlavi, invited Tagore to Iran in 1932. On his journeys and lecture tours Tagore attempted to spread the ideal of uniting East and West. While in Japan he wrote: "The Japanese do not waste their energy in useless screaming and quarreling, and because there is no waste of energy it is not found wanting when required. This calmness and fortitude of body and mind is part of their national self-realization."

Tagore wrote his most important works in Bengali, but he often translated his poems into English. At the age of 70, Tagore took up painting. He was also a composer, setting hundreds of poems to music. Many of his poems are actually songs and inseparable from their music. Tagore's "Our Golden Bengal" became the National Anthem of Bangladesh. Only hours before he died on August 7, in 1941, Tagore dictated his last poem. His written production, still not completely collected, fills nearly 30 substantial volumes. Tagore remained a well-known and popular author in the West until the end of the 1920s.

TAGORE WROTE A DESCRIPTION OF HAPPINESS IN THIS LIFE WHICH BECAME A SPIRITUAL RITE OF PASSAGE FOR ME AND THE THEME OF MY THIRD PUBLISHED BOOK, "MY GREATEST JOYS ON MY WAY HOME."

The content of what Tagore wrote:

"I went to sleep and dreamed

That *Life was happiness*;

I woke up and saw

That *Life was service*;

I served and I discovered

That *in service*

Is found Happiness."

I have kept this poem (in Spanish) taped to my bedroom door for years.

Padre Pio

CHAPTER 20
PADRE PIO, BILOCATION
AND THE ODOR OF SANCTITY

Francesco Forgione of Pietrelcina is also known as Padre Pio. He was born to a southern Italian farm family, the son of

Grazio, a shepherd. At age 15 he entered the novitiate of the Capuchin friars in Morcone, and joined the order at age 19. He suffered several health problems, and at one point his family thought he had tuberculosis. He was ordained at age 22 on 10 August 1910.

While praying before a cross, he received the stigmata on September 20, 1918, the first priest ever to be so blessed.

Among the most remarkable of the documented cases of bilocation was the Padre's appearance in the air over San Giovanni Rotondo during World War II. While southern Italy remained in Nazi hands, American bombers were given the job of attacking the city of San Giovanni Rotondo. However, when they appeared over the city and prepared to unload their munitions, a brown-robed Friar appeared before their aircraft. All attempts to release the bombs failed. In this way, Padre Pio kept his promise to the citizens that their town would be spared. Later on, when an American airbase was established at Foggia a few miles away, one of the pilots of this incident visited the friary and found to his surprise, the little friar he had seen in the air that day over San Giovanni.

As word spread, especially after American soldiers brought home stories of Padre Pio following WWII, the priest himself became a point of pilgrimage for both the pious and the curious. He would hear confessions by the hour, reportedly able to read the consciences of those who held back. Reportedly able to bilocate, levitate, and heal by touch. Founded the House for the Relief of Suffering in 1956, a hospital that serves 60,000 a year. In the 1920's he started a series of prayer groups that continue today with over 400,000 members worldwide.

As to how Padre Pio, with God's help, accomplished such feats, the closest he ever came to an explanation of bilocation was to say that it occurred "*by an extension of his personality.*"

For the good of souls, Our Lord gave the Venerable Padre Pio of Pietrelcina many gifts, amongst these the gift of bilocation, which enables a person to be present in two places at the same time.

Bilocation, however, must not be confused as some do with *ubiquity*, which means omnipresence, namely being present everywhere at the same time, which belongs only to God.

His canonization miracle involved the cure of Matteo Pio Colella, age 7, the son of a doctor who works in the House for Relief of Suffering, the hospital in San Giovanni Rotondo founded by Padre Pio. On the night of 20 June 2000, Matteo was admitted to the intensive care unit of the hospital with meningitis. By morning doctors had lost hope for him as nine of the boy's internal organs had ceased to give signs of life. That night, during a prayer vigil attended by Matteo's mother and some Capuchin friars of Padre Pio's monastery, the child's condition improved suddenly. When he awoke from the coma, Matteo said that he had seen an elderly man with a white beard and a long, brown habit, who said to him: "Don't worry, you will soon be cured." The miracle was approved by the Congregation and Pope John Paul II on December 20, 2001. Padre Pio was canonized on June 16, 2002 by Pope John Paul II.

I first heard of Padre Pio when I was a young Pastor at St. Bernadette Church in Dearborn. The phenomenon of bilocation and stigmatism to me were remarkable gifts attributed to Padre Pio. His appearances on various continents are attested by numerous eye witnesses, who either saw him or smelled the odors characteristically associated with his presence, described by some as roses and by others as tobacco. The phenomenon of odor (sometimes called the odor of sanctity) is itself well established in Padre Pio's case. The odor was especially strong from the blood coming from his wounds. Investigation showed that he used absolutely no fragrances or anything that could produce these odors. The odors often occurred when people called upon his intercession in prayer.

About this time in my life, I was working closely with the Holy Spirit and the Lord Jesus, who were introducing me to many spiritual Rites of Passage, each experience raising my level of spiritual awareness. At one point, I asked the question: is there anything I can do, while I am sleeping, to help other people. I was thinking more of saying a special prayer for others just before going to sleep. The Holy Spirit recommended doing *Rescue Work* while sleeping. Did He mean to *bilocate* just as Padre Pio did? No! Not at all! He meant that while my body is asleep, I could spiritually leave my body (called an Out-of-the-body experience, or known as an OBE). I did not quite understand. I was told by my Divine Guides that I could prepare people about to die by ministering to them beforehand. This action assists helpers on the other side welcoming the individual to the world of spirit much smoother and more gracefully. That is what was called Rescue Work.

From that point on, I would find myself on the street, at an ICU bed in a hospital awaiting death, in a home or even at a bar administering the Sacraments or simply praying with the dying person, who generally called for help. At first, it was an interesting Ministry, but after several days, it was wearing me out. If it were an accident, I would hear a "Pow! Or Bam!" And I would find myself at the scene of a horrible and bloody tragedy. I would get back to sleep and another accident occurred. After about three weeks, I had to stop that project. It was not bilocation in the way that Padre Pio accomplished. He was active in both places. I needed my sleep and could not continue being awakened so often, every night.

MY SPIRITUAL RITE OF PASSAGE: BILOCATION WAS REAL AND A SPECIAL GIFT OF GOD TO PADRE PIO. IN MY BRIEF RESCUE WORK I DID NOT BILOCATE, BUT LEARNED THAT WE CAN LEAVE THE BODY ASLEEP WHILE THE SPIRIT IS FREE.

CHAPTER 20
A COURSE IN MIRACLES
HOW IT WAS WRITTEN

I first heard of "A Course in Miracles" when a lady stopped at Holy Trinity Rectory where I was Pastor and gave me a set of the three books that make up "A Course in Miracles". She said it was a gift from the Holy Spirit. A week later, I received a telephone call from a friend in Seattle, Washington. She said that while they were praying as a group, she was told by the Holy Spirit that Fr. Jay Samonie should be studying "A Course in Miracles."

One week later, I attended a Conference at the Cayce Foundation. I was unaware that Dr. Kenneth Wapnick and Judith Skutch were giving a talk on "A Course In Miracles". They happened to be the foremost advocates and teachers of "A Course in Miracles." All of this happened within a three week period. How could I *not* feel that this was a direct message from the Holy Spirit!

When I returned home, I immediately gathered a group together to study "A Course In Miracles". During one of the sessions, Teresa Blanchard joined our group. She was very well versed in the Course.

Later, she and I began teaching and guiding discussions about it. We conducted our sessions about "A Course in Miracles" for five years at Holy Trinity Church. We often had over one hundred participants in attendance. I have continued to study the Course and try to apply it to my daily life.

Just how did A Course In Miracles come about?

It began with the sudden decision of two people to join in a common goal. Their names were Helen Schucman and William Thetford, Professors of Medical Psychology at Columbia University's College of Physicians and Surgeons in New York City. They were anything but spiritual. Their relationship with each other was difficult and often strained. They were concerned with personal and professional acceptance and status. In general, they had considerable investment in the values of the world. Their lives were hardly in accord with anything that the Course advocates. Helen, the one who received the material, describes herself:

"Psychologist, educator, conservative in theory and atheistic in belief, I was working in a prestigious and highly academic setting. And then something happened that triggered a chain of events I could never have predicted. The head of my department unexpectedly announced that he was tired of the angry and aggressive feelings our attitudes reflected, and concluded that, there must be another way. As if on cue, I agreed to help him find it. Apparently, this Course is the other way."

Although their intention was serious, they had great difficulty in starting out on their joint venture. But they had unwittingly given the Holy Spirit the "little willingness" that, as the Course itself was to emphasize again and again, is sufficient to enable Him to use any situation for His purposes and provide it with His power.

To continue Helen's first-person account of how it happened:

"Three startling months preceded the actual writing, during which time Bill suggested that I write down the highly symbolic dreams and descriptions of the strange images that were coming to me. Although I had grown more accustomed to the unexpected by that time, I was still very surprised when I wrote, *This is a course in miracles.* That was my introduction to the Voice.

It made no sound, but seemed to be giving me a kind of rapid, inner dictation which I took down in a shorthand notebook. The writing was never automatic. It could be interrupted at any time and later picked up again. It made me very uncomfortable, but it never seriously occurred to me to stop. It seemed to be a special assignment I had somehow, somewhere agreed to complete. It represented a truly collaborative venture between Bill and myself, and much of its significance, I am sure, lies in that.

I would take down what the Voice "said" and read it to him the next day and he typed it from my dictation. I expect he had his special assignment, too. Without his encouragement and support, I would never have been able to fulfill mine. The whole process took about seven years. The Text came first, then the Workbook for Students and, finally, the Manual for Teachers. Only a few minor changes have been made. Chapter titles and subheadings have been inserted in the Text, and some of the more personal references that occurred at the beginning have been omitted. Otherwise the material is substantially unchanged."

The names of the collaborators in the recording of the Course do not appear on the cover, because the Course can and should stand on its own. It is not intended to become the basis for another cult. MY SPIRITUAL RITE OF PASSAGE: A COURSE IN MIRACLES' PURPOSE IS TO PROVIDE A WAY IN WHICH SOME PEOPLE WILL BE ABLE TO FIND THEIR OWN INTERNAL TEACHER.

WHAT IS A COURSE IN MIRACLES?

As its title implies, the Course is arranged throughout as a teaching device. It consists of three books: a 622-page Text, a 478-page Workbook for Students and an 88-page Manual for Teachers. The order in which students choose to use the books and the ways in which they study them, depend on their particular needs and preferences.

The curriculum the Course proposes is carefully conceived and is explained, step by step, at both the theoretical and practical levels. It emphasizes *application* rather than theory and *experience* rather than theology. *ANOTHER* SPIRITUAL RITE OF PASSAGE*: ACIM SPECIFICALLY STATES THAT "A UNIVERSAL THEOLOGY IS IMPOSSIBLE, BUT A UNIVERSAL EXPERIENCE IS NOT ONLY POSSIBLE BUT NECESSARY."* (Manual, p. 77)

We do not have to look very far to witness this principle here on earth. Theology has never been more divided and openly hostile, since the beginning of the human race. Ireland is a good example, the Arabs and the Jews another, constant conflicts among the divided African nations and many small but hostile war-like rivalries between neighboring tribes. The Christian religions, in general, are also seriously divided between the fundamental and the liberal, and verbal conflict between those embracing religious or spiritual systems. Both sides around the world never stop, yet they may be all having some religious experience according to their belief in God, Allah, Yahweh or Buddha. It never stops.

Although Christian in statement, the Course deals with universal spiritual themes. It emphasizes that it is but one version of the universal curriculum. There are many others, this one differing from them only in form. They all lead to God in the end.

The Text is largely theoretical and sets forth the concepts on which the Course's thought system is based. Its ideas contain the foundation for the Workbook's lessons. Without the practical application the Workbook provides, the Text would remain largely a series of abstractions, which would hardly suffice to bring about the thought reversal at which the Course aims.

The Workbook includes 365 lessons, one for each day of the year. It is not necessary, however, to do the lessons at that tempo and one might want to remain with a particularly appealing lesson for more than one day. The instructions urge only that not more than one lesson a day should be attempted. The practical nature of the Workbook is underscored by the introduction to its lessons, which emphasizes experience through application rather than a prior commitment to a spiritual goal.

Some of the ideas the workbook presents you will find hard to believe, and others may seem to be quite startling. This does not matter. You are merely asked to apply the ideas as you are directed to do. You are not asked to judge them at all. You are asked only to use them. It is their use that will give them meaning to you and will show you that they are true.

Remember only this; you need not believe the ideas, you need not accept them and you need not even welcome them. Some of them you may actively resist. None of this will matter or decrease their efficacy.

But do not allow yourself to make exceptions in applying the ideas the workbook contains and whatever your reactions to the ideas may be, use them. Nothing more than that is required (Workbook, p. 2).

Finally, the Manual for Teachers, which is written in question and answer form, provides answers to some of the more likely questions a student might ask. It also includes a clarification of a number of the terms the Course uses, explaining them within the theoretical framework of the Text.

The Course makes no claim to finality, nor are the Workbook lessons intended to bring the student's learning to completion. At the end, the reader is left in the hands of his or her own Internal Teacher, Who will direct all subsequent learning as He sees fit. While the Course is comprehensive in scope, truth cannot be limited to any finite form, as is clearly recognized in the statement at the end of the Workbook:

"This Course is a beginning, not an end...No more specific lessons are assigned, for there is no more need of them. Henceforth, hear but the Voice for God...He will direct your efforts, telling you exactly what to do, how to direct your mind, and when to come to Him in silence, asking for His sure direction and His certain Word." (Workbook, p. 487).

WHAT A COURSE IN MIRACLES SAYS:

Nothing real can be threatened.

Nothing unreal exists.

Herein lies the peace of God.

I think about this every day, because we are confronted constantly with what is Real and Eternal versus what is unreal and temporary. This is how A Course in Miracles begins. It makes a fundamental distinction between the Real and the unreal; between Knowledge and perception. Knowledge is Truth, under one law, the law of love or God. Truth is unalterable, eternal and unambiguous. Absolute Truth may not be recognized, but it cannot be changed. It applies to everything that God created, and only what He created is Real. It is beyond learning, because it is beyond time and process. It has no opposite; no beginning and no end. It merely is.

The world of perception, on the other hand, is the world of time, of change, of beginnings and endings. It is based on interpretation, not on facts. It is the world of birth and death, founded on the belief in scarcity, loss, separation and death. It is learned rather than given, selective in what it perceives, unstable in its functioning, and inaccurate in its interpretations.

From Knowledge and perception respectively, two distinct thought systems arise which are opposite in every respect. In the realm of Knowledge no thoughts exist apart from God, because God and His Creation share one Will. The world of perception, however, is made by the belief in opposites and separate wills, in perpetual conflict with each other and with God. What perception sees and hears appears to be real, because it permits into one's awareness only what conforms to the wishes of the perceiver. This leads to a world of illusions, a world which needs constant defense precisely because it is not real. This represents the world in which we live!

When you have been caught in the world of perception you are caught in a dream. You cannot escape without help, because everything your senses show merely witnesses to the reality of the dream. God has provided the Answer, the only Way out, the true Helper. It is the function of His Voice, His Holy Spirit, to mediate between the two worlds. He can do this because, while on the one hand He knows the Truth, He also recognizes our illusions, but without believing in them.

It is the Holy Spirit's goal to help us escape from the dream world by teaching us how to reverse our thinking and unlearn our mistakes. Forgiveness is the Holy Spirit's great learning aid in bringing about this thought reversal. However, the Course has its own definition of what forgiveness really is, just as it defines the world in its own way.

The world we see merely reflects our own internal frame of reference — the dominant ideas, wishes and emotions in our minds. "Projection makes perception" (Text, p. 445). We look inside first, decide the kind of world we want to see and then project that world outside, making it the truth as we see it. We make it true by our interpretations of what it is we are seeing. If we are using perception to justify our own mistakes —— our anger, our impulses to attack, our lack of love in whatever form it may take —- we will see a world of evil, destruction, malice, envy and despair. It is a world based on fear and separation from God.

All this we must learn to forgive, not because we are being "good" and "charitable," but because what we are seeing is not true. We have distorted the world by our twisted defenses and are, therefore, seeing what is not there. As we learn to recognize our perceptual errors, we also learn to look past them or "forgive." At the same time we are forgiving ourselves, looking past our distorted self-concepts to the Self That God created in us and as us. I saw a movie on television last night, "Remember the Titans", first aired in the year 2000. My eyes became a little teary when I saw the black and white football players after being "we" versus "them", forget about color and embrace each other like brothers and sisters of the same team and family. It reminded me of our true Home in God's Eternal Kingdom, where all is one; where there is no sense of separation. That movie touched my soul.

Sin is defined as "lack of love" (Text, p. 11). Since love is all there is, sin in the sight of the Holy Spirit is a mistake to be corrected, rather than an evil to be punished. Our sense of inadequacy, weakness and incompletion comes from the strong investment in the "scarcity principle" that governs the whole world of illusions. From that point of view, we seek in others what we feel is wanting in ourselves. We "love" another in order to get something ourselves. That, in fact, is what passes for love in the dream world. There can be no greater mistake than that, for love is incapable of asking for anything.

Only minds can really join, and whom God has joined no man can put asunder

(Text, p. 356). It is, however, only at the level of the Christ Mind that true union is possible and has, in fact, never been lost. The "little I" seeks to enhance itself by external approval, external possessions and external "Love." The Self that God created needs nothing. It is forever complete, safe, loved and loving. It seeks to share rather than to get; to extend rather than project. It has no needs and wants to join with others out of their mutual awareness of abundance.

The special relationships of the world are destructive, selfish and childishly egocentric. Yet, if given to the Holy Spirit, these relationships can become the holiest things on earth —— the miracles that point the way to the return to Heaven. The world uses its special relationships as a final weapon of exclusion and a demonstration of separateness. The Holy Spirit transforms them into perfect lessons in forgiveness and in awakening from the dream. Each one is an opportunity to let perceptions be healed and errors corrected. Each one is given another chance to forgive oneself by forgiving the other. And each one becomes still another invitation to the Holy Spirit and to the remembrance of God.

Perception is a function of the body and, therefore, represents a limit on awareness. Perception sees through the body's eyes and hears through the body's ears. It evokes the limited responses which the body makes. The body appears to be largely self-motivated and independent, yet it actually responds only to the intentions of the mind. If the mind wants to use it for attack in any form, it becomes prey to sickness, age and decay. If the mind accepts the Holy Spirit's purpose for it instead, it becomes a useful way of communicating with others, invulnerable as long as it is needed, and to be gently laid aside when its use is over. Of itself, the body is neutral, as is everything in the world of perception. Whether it is used for the goals of the ego or for the Holy Spirit depends entirely on what the mind wants.

The opposite of seeing through the body's eyes is the *Vision of Christ*, which reflects strength rather than weakness, unity rather than separation and love rather than fear. The opposite of hearing through the body's ears is communication through the Voice for God, the Holy Spirit, which abides in each one of us. His Voice seems distant and difficult to hear because the ego, which speaks for the little, separated self, seems to be much louder. This is actually reversed. The Holy Spirit speaks with unmistakable clarity and overwhelming appeal. No one who does not choose to identify with the body could possibly be deaf to His messages of release and hope, nor could he fail to accept joyously the vision of Christ in glad exchange for his miserable picture of himself.

Christ's vision is the Holy Spirit's gift, God's alternative to the illusion of separation and to the belief in the reality of sin, guilt and death. It is the one correction for all errors of perception; the reconciliation of the seeming opposites on which this world is based. Its kindly *light* shows all things from another point of view, reflecting the thought system that arises from true Knowledge and making the return to God not only possible, but inevitable.

What was regarded as injustices done to one by someone else, now becomes a call for help and for union. Sin, guilt, sickness and attack are seen as misperceptions calling for a remedy through gentleness and love. Defenses are laid down, because where there is no attack there is no need for them. Our brothers' or sisters' needs become our own, because they are taking the journey with us as we go to God. Without us, they would lose their way. Without them, we could never find our own.

Forgiveness is unknown in Heaven, where the need for it would be inconceivable. However, in this world, forgiveness is a necessary correction for all the mistakes that we have made. To offer forgiveness is the only way for us to have it, for it reflects the law of Heaven that giving and receiving are the same. Heaven is the natural state of all the Children of God as He created them. Such is their Reality forever. It has not changed, because it has not been forgotten.

Forgiveness is the means by which we will remember. Through forgiveness the thinking of the world is reversed. The forgiven world becomes the gate of Heaven, because by its mercy we can at last forgive ourselves. Holding no one prisoner to guilt, we become free. Acknowledging Christ in all our brothers and sisters, we recognize His Presence in ourselves. Forgetting all our misperceptions and with nothing from the past to hold us back, we can remember God. Beyond this, learning cannot go. When we are ready, God Himself will take the final step in our return to Him.

And we shall return here no more! We will be awakened and taken Home to God's Eternal Kingdom (Which we had never really left) and our joy will be beyond anything we could possibly imagine in this life!

To order additional copies of "The Rite of Passage: Describing the Spiritual Rites of Passage of Rev. Jay J. Samonie, Ph.D." or any of the other books by Father Jay Samonie, please complete the order form on the following page and mail form with check payable to:

Rev Jay Samonie
34666 Spring Valley Drive
Westland MI 48185-9457

Father Jay is pleased to join with Frameworks Gallery in Plymouth, Michigan to reproduce his artwork. With 30 years experience in art and framing, Frameworks Gallery, through its digital imaging division, Custom Arts, is a leading producer of giclée fine art prints in southeast Michigan. For more information please visit the web site:

www.fatherjay.org

Name (Please Print)			
Address			
City, State, Zip			
Telephone (Include Area Code)			

Qty	Title	Price	Extend
	On My Way Home	$14.95	
	Reflections On My Way Home	$14.95	
	My Greatest Joys On My Way	$14.95	
	The Holy Spirit: Our Divine Companion Guiding Us On Our Way Home	$19.95	
	"The Rite of Passage: Describing the Spiritual Rites of Passage of Rev. Jay J. Samonie, Ph.D.	$14.95	

Subtotal	
Michigan Residents (Add 6% Sales Tax)	
Shipping & Handling ($3 Per Book)	
Total Amount Enclosed	